THE ROYAL HORTICULTURAL SOCIETY
PRACTICAL GUIDES

HANGING
BASKETS

DAVID JOYCE

DORLING KINDERSLEY
LONDON • NEW YORK • SYDNEY
www.dk.com

LONDON, NEW YORK, MUNICH, MELBOURNE, DELHI

Project Editor Jennifer Jones
Art Editor Alison Donovan

Series Editor Gillian Roberts
Series Art Editor Stephen Josland

Senior Managing Editor Mary-Clare Jerram
Managing Art Editor Lee Griffiths

DTP Designer Louise Paddick

Production Mandy Inness

First published in Great Britain in 2000
Reprinted 2002
by Dorling Kindersley Limited,
80 Strand, London WC2R 0RL

A Penguin Company

Copyright © 2000 Dorling Kindersley Limited, London

A CIP catalogue record for this book is available from the British Library.

ISBN 0 7513 47167

Reproduced by Colourscan, Singapore
Printed and bound by Star Standard Industries, Singapore

See our complete catalogue at
www.dk.com

CONTENTS

SUCCESSFUL HANGING BASKETS

CLASSIC DISPLAYS

THE ESSENTIAL COMPONENTS of a hanging basket are simply a small collection of plants growing in a suspended container, but in a short season they can make a wonderful floating confection of flowers and foliage. The eye-catching effect of a well-planted hanging basket transforms porches, doorways, and blank areas of the garden, and enlivens conservatory displays.

PLANT-FILLED BASKETS

A successful hanging basket is like a superb cascading flower arrangement but one in which the plants do most of the arranging themselves. The key to achieving this apparently artless effect is to make a selection of compatible plants, including some that trail or fling out lax stems, so that when the planting is in its prime the basket itself is lost to view.

The main season for hanging baskets is summer, when a wide range of plants will give colourful displays that last for many weeks. Some of the most popular garden and container plants, among them petunias, pelargoniums, and verbenas, are well suited to hanging baskets; but hardly less important than flowering plants are those with good foliage, such as ivies and *Helichrysum petiolare*. These give fullness to mixtures, temper strong colours, and make peace between plants whose colours might clash.

Even several herbs can do well in baskets (*see p.73*), and for adventurous gardeners there are numerous beautiful but less familiar ornamentals, such as *Begonia sutherlandii*, that make it possible to have outdoor or indoor displays throughout the year.

► ADVENTUROUS MIXTURE
The silvered foliage of Lamium maculatum *helps bind together an imaginative combination that includes vivid, large-flowered tuberous begonias, verbenas, yellow-flowered* Bidens ferulifolia, *and an airy diascia.*

◄ HARMONIOUS CASCADE *Pale Surfinia petunias blend with purple verbenas and* Scaevola aemula.

THE INVISIBLE BASKET

Beneath the casual tumbling growth of a successful hanging basket there is usually a metal or plastic-coated wire frame holding the compost on which the plants rely for their supplies of water and nutrients. Since the conventional basket is functional rather than pleasing to the eye, it pays to take trouble to plant it so that it is well concealed. You might expect all the planting to be done at the top, as is the case with most other containers. However, even fast-growing plants, as are many of the popular summer-flowering annuals, may not make enough growth in a season or hug the basket close enough to mask it. The trick is to plant at the top and through the sides. The gaps in the frame allow young plants to be inserted, and the liner can be slit, punched through, or teased apart, depending on the material. Planting through the sides is best done as the basket is being filled with compost; be sure to bed the roots well into the compost. A useful formula is to plant trailing and

---

The trick is to plant at the top and through the sides

---

lax plants, such as lobelias and the silvery foliage plant *Helichrysum petiolare*, on the sides and at the rim while crowning the basket with clump-forming or more upright plants, such as zonal pelargoniums, busy Lizzies, and pansies.

▲ IVY SOLO
Ivies are versatile foliage plants for hanging baskets, their trailing stems providing an elegant base for flowers. Planted alone, they form pretty cascades.

▶ LAYERED EFFECT
In these paired baskets the vivid flowers of tuberous begonias crown a layered planting that includes lobelias, busy Lizzies, and trails of Lysimachia nummularia *'Aurea'.*

► DELICATE PINKS
A medley of pinks – from the merest whisper of colour to a clear lavender-pink – brings together ivy-leaved pelargoniums, verbenas, diascias, and lobelias. This arrangement would be pretty displayed beside a pastel-coloured door.

CHOICE OF EFFECT

The range of hues for a summer display of flowers extends from the softest pastels to intensely deep and vibrant colours; the choice is up to you. Bear in mind, though, that as hanging baskets are intended mainly to decorate areas close to the house, or inside it, a coordinated approach to colour will produce the best results. Complement pale-coloured architectural features, such as white doors and window frames, with plantings in harmonious blends of watercolour tints. A suitable display might combine lobelias, petunias, verbenas, and *Helichrysum petiolare* to create a delicate medley of blue, pink, and lilac flowers softened by grey-green foliage. It is just as easy to create dramatic focal points using bursts of one or more bright colours. Tuberous begonias, which come in a wide range of vivid colours, are ideal for these effects.

Other seasons are shorter and the colour choice more limited, but polyanthus and winter-flowering pansies still furnish a delectable selection. In any season, there is always the option of a restrained effect using foliage plants, such as ferns and ivies.

◄ AIRY DISPLAY
This classic hanging-basket mixture, standing out against a white weatherboard house, has a central clump of red begonias, floss flowers, and Senecio cineraria *surrounded by a swirl of fuchsias, lobelias, and ivy-leaved pelargoniums.*

VARIATIONS ON A THEME

THERE ARE MANY CONTAINERS that you can use instead of standard hanging baskets. These range from hand-thrown terracotta pots and solid plastic hanging containers, in a range of designs, to wall-mounted planters, such as hayracks and purpose-made terracotta half-bowls. There is also scope – if you have a flair for improvisation – in commandeered household containers and recycled items that add their own character to planted displays.

HANGING POTS

The individuality of a hanging terracotta container and its sympathetic colouring make it an attractive alternative to hanging baskets in most locations. However, such clay pots are heavy, especially when filled with compost and plants, so a really stout support is essential. Solid plastic hanging containers have the advantage of being lightweight, and they are available in a range of colours with a matt or smooth finish. The least conspicuous are those with a matt surface in dark colours or in terracotta. Some come with drip-tray attachments; an added refinement are those that incorporate a reservoir in the base, a wick taking water from it to keep the compost moist. The reservoirs of these "self-watering" containers must be topped up, but they need watering less often.

One disadvantage of purpose-made pots is that their solid construction does not

▲ SELF-WATERING POT
Jostling pansies fill a plastic container that has a water reservoir and wick to keep compost moist. The container's edge could be softened by the addition of trailing plants, such as ivies.

▶ BIRDCAGE DISPLAY
An open birdcage framework draws attention to an attractive planting, which includes a fuchsia and busy Lizzies. The plants are held in a large pot placed in the base of the cage.

normally allow for planting in the sides – a distinct feature of metal frame or plastic-coated wire baskets. Sometimes the quality of a container makes it worth being seen as an important part of the display. Even then, planting should at least soften the hard edge of the rim, and in most cases it is best to make generous use of lax and trailing plants to achieve this.

WALL-MOUNTED CONTAINERS

Where space is limited, where there is no overhead support, and where there is a blank wall that could be improved by a planted display, wall-mounted containers are often a good alternative to hanging baskets. Small terracotta wall pots suspended from a nail or hook make appealing decorative details. An imaginatively planted cluster of ordinary pots, plastic, or terracotta, suspended in metal brackets, can transform the dullest corners. For larger displays, a hayrack container provides more scope. It consists of a metal framework that holds a liner filled with compost, and comes in various

▲ MODERN DESIGN
An eye-catching combination of foliage and flowering plants complements an unusually shaped terracotta pot, but it will need careful watering to ensure a healthy, long-lived display.

▲ MINIATURE WALL POT
A slowly spreading houseleek (Sempervivum) revels in the good drainage provided by this small terracotta wall pot.

◄ TIGHT CORNER
Busy Lizzies, begonias, fuchsias, petunias, and other bright flowers fill a wall-mounted container shaped to fit a right-angled corner.

sizes. There are also shapes to suit corners. Treat like conventional hanging baskets, concealing the structure by planting through the front as well as at the top.

IMPROVISED CONTAINERS

Many household items make characterful suspended containers for a conservatory or outside. Ideally, choose items with a pierced or mesh-like structure so that, like conventional hanging baskets, they can be lined to hold compost and plants but allow excess moisture to drain away. When filled the container should not be so heavy that it is difficult to support, but it must be large and deep enough to hold sufficient compost to sustain plants and give them anchorage. A depth of 15–30cm (6–12in) is ideal. Household items that fit the bill include various wirework containers: egg baskets, salad baskets, and fruit or vegetable baskets are obvious choices. So, too, is a colander – perhaps one in bright enamel to establish the colour theme of a display. Wicker baskets come in a wide range of shapes and textures. To minimize water damage, treat them inside and out with marine varnish or similar preservative.

▲ WALL-MOUNTED BASKET
Wickerwork containers come in a range of interesting textures and colours that go well with plants. This wall-mounted basket is planted with a yellow-flowered kalanchoe.

▼ HAYRACK FOR SHADE
A bright mix of busy Lizzies, begonias, and fuchsias brings a splash of colour to a semi-shaded position. This hayrack is lined with sphagnum moss, but other options for liners that are more environmentally friendly include those made from coir fibre.

◀ BRIGHT COLANDER
Long-flowering osteospermums in white and shades of purple and trailing variegated ivies make a good match for a large colander of metallic lustre used as a hanging basket. Line the colander as for a standard hanging basket.

▼ YELLOW SPLASH
An old-fashioned bottle carrier is easy to adapt as a suspended container for plants in pots to give seasonal displays. Here, the individual compartments are filled with French marigolds.

Buckets, preferably made of lightweight zinc, can be adapted as containers by drilling holes in the base for drainage. Some items, such as bottle carriers, are best used as suspended containers for collections of small pots. Items that do not have drainage holes can be used indoors as suspended trays for container-grown plants. A successful conventional hanging basket is usually hidden by its planting, but plant unusual containers in a way that shows off their individuality.

ADDING DECORATION

For decisive colour effects, paint containers. A well-chosen colour or mixture of colours can transform a nondescript container, turning it into an important element in a coordinated scheme. Bear in mind the setting when choosing colours, perhaps selecting hues to match or contrast with architectural features, such as windows and doors. When you have decided on your

scheme, you can use either an oil-based or water-based paint, and then finish with a coat or two of clear marine varnish to protect the surface from the weather. Follow through with a planting that produces quiet harmonies or bold challenges.

SITING AND GROUPING DISPLAYS

THE CHOICE OF LOCATIONS for hanging baskets and wall-mounted containers on and near buildings and elsewhere in the garden is extremely wide, limited only by the availability of suitable supports. Always decide on a site before preparing your container, and sort out from the start practical matters, such as the type of support required, whether and how much clearance you need to allow for pedestrian traffic, and if dripping water will cause a problem.

PRIME SITES

A good position is one that is sheltered from strong winds, gives the display prominence, and fills a gap or creates a focal point in an area that is otherwise uninteresting. Hanging baskets suspended from brackets, or wall-mounted containers, make a particularly cheerful display when positioned on a wall opposite a door or window or when announcing the entrance to a house. Remember, though, that a hanging basket should always be a visual

delight but never get in the way. Containers also need to be positioned so that watering and grooming can be carried out easily; for better access, baskets can be hung from a pulley attachment (*see p.60*). Wind is not likely to dislodge a well-secured basket, but constant buffeting may cause damage to plants, particularly those with brittle stems and conservatory plants that have been moved outdoors for the summer. The most serious threat posed by wind to all plants in containers is its drying effect.

COLOURFUL SHADE
Few flowering plants suitable for hanging baskets are more consistently effective in shade than busy Lizzies. The strong colours of some kinds have a startling brilliance, but there are also selections with soft and delicate tones.

▲ COOL GREEN
Areas that are in shade present a challenge. Foliage plants, especially ferns and ivies with distinctive silver or gold markings, are a good choice.

◄ SUN LOVERS
Petunias and Bidens ferulifolia *thrive in a sunny spot. Both plants flower for several months in summer.*

SUN OR SHADE

Many popular plants suitable for hanging baskets are of an easy-going character, thriving in both full sun and semi-shade – petunias, for example, although happiest in full sun, will also flower in partial shade.

> A hanging basket should always be a visual delight but never get in the way

However, the number of flowering plants that will put on a good display in moderate to heavy shade is limited. Many will grow in a well-lit spot with no direct sunlight but will then tend to produce leaves at the expense of flowers. For colour in shade, few plants can match the performance of busy Lizzies, which have a long and colourful season. Among the best plants for positions in full shade are those, such as ferns and variegated ivies, that rely on foliage for their ornamental effect.

▲ SUMMER OUTING
Tradescantias are attractive trailing foliage plants. They are good year-round in the home or conservatory, but can be hung outdoors in summer.

SINGLES AND GROUPS

A solitary hanging basket or wall-mounted container can easily stand alone, either as a powerful eye-catcher or simply as a pleasing detail. Place baskets so that they seem to be the element that completes the picture. The key focal points in a garden lie along or at the end of the main axes and sight lines, including those running from the interior through doors and windows to the garden outside. You might use a single hanging basket at the centre of an arch or marking the right-angled junction of two walls. A hayrack container fixed to a wall or fence at the end of a path makes a strong focal point to close the vista.

A matched pair of containers placed either side of a feature is the simplest kind of symmetrical arrangement, and is a highly effective and decorative way of flanking a door or window. Although the planting does not have to be strictly symmetrical, the pairing will seem out of joint if shape, colour, and tone are not balanced over all. Pairs can form the basis of a more elaborate symmetrical arrangement, including pots on the ground as well as hanging baskets. Small wall-mounted containers lend themselves to grouped arrangements. Seen from inside the house, a collection of pots centred on an otherwise bare patio wall makes it seem purpose-built to show off a seasonal display of plants. To give substance to the display, group other containers below it, either at ground level or on raised staging. The same planting can be repeated in each pot, different plantings can be combined in a pattern, or a random arrangement of different plantings can create a high-spirited mix.

▲ PAIRED BASKETS
An elegant white façade is perfectly complemented by two matching hanging baskets either side of the doorway filled with a frothy mixture dominated by petunias.

► TIERED DISPLAY
Symmetrically arranged containers, including hanging baskets planted with fuchsias and lobelias, give colour and interest to a doorway.

◀ EYE-CATCHER
This richly planted hanging basket makes a vivid focal point at the centre of an archway.

▲ LOW BASKETS
Hanging baskets that are hung low can be enjoyed from inside and do not cut out the light.

VARYING THE HEIGHT

At the usual height for a hanging basket – 1.5–2.2m (5–7ft) above ground level – it is reasonably easy to water and groom plants, and the container is well positioned to catch the eye of a standing person. Even so, there are often good practical and aesthetic reasons to vary the height. A range of heights gives interest to a grouping of several baskets and containers. High planting may be necessary to provide clearance for pedestrian traffic,

say at the centre of an arch. A position well above head height adds to the dramatic effect of a luxuriously planted hanging basket. Hanging a basket low brings the display closer to the viewer, and is a practical option in front of a window where it might otherwise block the light. When containers are hung low the sides are less visible, an advantage when undistinguished pots are planted with upright and bushy ornamentals, as in spring displays (*see pp.22–23*).

COLOURFUL WALKWAY
A wooden pergola spanning a long walk is enlivened by a measured arrangement of baskets. Summer bedding plants such as begonias, busy Lizzies, lobelias, and violas provide the bright colours of this extravagant display.

INDOOR DISPLAYS

HANGING BASKETS AND OTHER KINDS of suspended containers provide an attractive way of growing a wide range of ornamentals indoors, including in conservatories. There is no sharp divide between plants for the open garden and those for indoors, but priority is usually given in the conservatory or home to plants that need a protected environment. Many of those that would not survive outdoors in winter can be moved outside in summer.

CONTAINERS AND PLANTS

Lax and trailing plants are the first choice for indoor displays, with a heavy reliance on perennial foliage plants. Many of the most striking are plants of tropical or subtropical origin. Orchids, no longer the preserve of specialists, are increasingly

> ## Lax and trailing plants are the first choice for indoor displays

popular for their exotic flowers. The hanging baskets and pots that are used outdoors are also suitable for indoor gardening, but greater emphasis is usually placed on the decorative effect of the container and its

support. Solid plastic hanging pots with drip-tray attachments prevent drip problems – ideally, reserve them for trailing plants that will cover up the functional-looking pot. A wooden slatted box (*see pp.36–39*) is favoured for orchids and is also suitable for ferns. The open structure of the box is ideally suited to orchids that naturally grow on the branches of trees and require plenty of air to reach their roots.

LIGHT, HUMIDITY, VENTILATION

In a well-designed conservatory the light levels are high enough for most plants and some shading may be necessary in summer. However, crowding and tall growth can affect light levels on the floor of the conservatory. So, too, can an excessive number of containers suspended from the

BRIGHT LIGHTS
The glass bowls of old lamps, imaginatively recycled, have been suspended from the roof of a conservatory and used as trays to hold pots of pelargoniums.

CHOICE SELECTION
Plants that have arching stems, like this succulent Kalanchoe manginii, *are ideal for displaying in a hanging basket. In spring, it bears drooping clusters of bell-shaped flowers.*

◀SUN OR SHADE
Busy Lizzies are an excellent choice as conservatory plants. They are shade tolerant, come in many colours, and will develop their flowers to unblemished perfection in the sheltered environment.

▼PARENT AND OFFSPRING
The spider plant, an undemanding choice for home or conservatory, has an elegantly casual way of producing numerous small replicas of itself, which shows well when it is grown in a hanging basket.

roof. In the home, light levels vary according to the size of windows and how far the container is hung from them. Many plants can thrive even though not in full sun, as long as they are in a well-lit position; but you have to strike a balance. If you favour plants by hanging them near windows, they will take light away from the rest of the room.

A large number of plants do best at humidity levels that are much higher than those of the average home. A water feature may be a practical way of lifting humidity levels in a conservatory, but in the house careful misting of containers, ensuring that spray drift does not damage furnishings, is usually the most effective way to counteract dryness. Water carefully to avoid drip marks.

Although plants dislike draughty positions in the house, good ventilation is important; in the conservatory, a small electric fan should be sufficient to ensure adequate air movement. The protected environment indoors favours some pests and you may have to take special measures to control them.

CHOICE OF PLANTS

To ENSURE THAT HANGING BASKETS make a strong impact, they need robust foliage and flowering plants that are quick to find their feet in a solo or mixed planting, speedily reach their full potential, and then continue to give value over weeks or months. The most popular plants for containers are excellent mixers, not taking over but able to stand their ground when growing in competition with other vigorous plants.

CATEGORIES OF PLANTS

The true annuals and other plants that achieve flowering maturity from seed or cuttings in a single season are the mainstay of summer displays. The best remain colourful for several months, particularly if they are deadheaded regularly to prolong flowering. A few perennials that are best known as foliage plants in the open garden are useful for bold effects when planted as mature specimens. The jagged bronze-purple leaves of *Heuchera micrantha* 'Palace Purple' make a really handsome dark clump. The upright growth of bulbs counts against them in hanging displays, but for spring baskets you can use short-stemmed kinds such as dwarf daffodils and tulips. Although woody plants are little used, there is scope for experimenting with dwarf shrubs. Young plants of variegated *Euonymus fortunei* are among the best evergreen foliage fillers.

▲ DISTINGUISHED GREY
Trailing Plecostachys
serpyllifolia *makes a subtle
partnership with mauve Swan
River daisies, but its grey
foliage also works well with
strong colours.*

▶ UPRIGHT AND TRAILING
*Dwarf tobacco plants make
an unusually strong upright
display. Their vertical thrust is
counterbalanced by low busy
Lizzies spreading over a skirt
of light blue lobelias.*

▲ GOOD MIXERS
A hanging basket is the ideal meeting place for good mixers – here, lobelias, pansies, pelargoniums, fuchsias, and begonias all contribute to a long summer display.

◀ RELIABLE COLOUR
Ivy-leaved and zonal pelargoniums are among the most reliable and rewarding plants for sunny summer displays. Their long season is prolonged if dead flowers are removed promptly.

TYPE OF GROWTH

A good shape for the finished planting of a light and airy hanging basket is a low and irregular dome topping a skirt of foliage and flowers. Avoid all lanky plants, as they cannot be integrated into a balanced display and are vulnerable to wind damage. A few short and stocky upright plants, such as zonal pelargoniums and upright begonias, can be used in the crown. But the true naturals for hanging baskets are plants of lax growth. Some that are low and spreading, including pansies and busy Lizzies, are good at the edge of baskets. This is the best place, too, for trailing fuchsias and several other trailing plants of rather stiff growth, among them *Scaevola aemula*. To mask the container itself, rely on really pliant plants, such as cascading lobelias, which can be planted through the basket liner.

GOOD TRAILING FOLIAGE

Glechoma hederacea 'Variegata' Long trailing stems and scalloped leaves with markings.
Hedera helix Common ivy is an outstanding trailing evergreen with many variations.
Helichrysum petiolare Excellent mixer, spreading and trailing stems carrying soft grey leaves.
Lotus berthelotii Coral gem, or parrot's beak, has pretty pea-like flowers and long trails of needle-like grey-green leaves.
Lysimachia nummularia 'Aurea' Golden creeping Jenny, with long trailing stems, has yellow-green leaves and yellow flowers.
Pelargonium 'L'Elégante' Ivy-leaved pelargonium, with cream-variegated foliage and white flowers.
Plecostachys serpyllifolia Lightweight shrub with silvery foliage.
Plectranthus forsteri 'Marginatus' Crisp white variegation.

SEASONAL OPTIONS

In cool climates, colourful half-hardy annuals and tender perennials make wonderful displays in summer until frost knocks them back. Frost also brings to an end the season for many edible plants. The choice among these is limited to plants of suitable growth and size. A dwarf bush tomato with a cascading habit, such as 'Tumbler', will reward you with a crop of flavoursome cherry tomatoes; alternatively, try growing an alpine strawberry such as 'Mignonette', which is suitable for a partially shaded spot. Herbs for the kitchen are always useful and some can be very decorative: favourites include thyme, marjoram, parsley, mint, sage, and rosemary. Try growing any of the above together or combine them with flowering annuals, which give extra colour and help to soften the overall planting.

In a relatively mild climate, where there is little risk of the compost in a basket being frozen for weeks or months at a time, displays outside the main summer season are feasible and particularly welcome.

Herbs for the kitchen are always useful and some can be very decorative

Where frosts come late, if at all, summer baskets will often remain colourful well into autumn. An unusual planting of perennials with, say, dwarf hostas, gives a true autumn effect, the leaves changing colour before they die down. Heavily berried gaultherias are splendid in large hayrack containers but, like most berrying plants, are too large for hanging baskets.

▲ SPRING HERB BASKET
Herbs, including lemon balm and parsley, make an unusual accompaniment to spring flowers such as double daisies, primulas, and violas.

► SUMMER RICHNESS
With regular deadheading, many annuals, including tobacco plants and nasturtiums, give a long summer season.

▲LATE WINTER COLOUR
*Variegated ivy softens the
outline of a hanging pot in
which an ornamental cabbage
is surrounded by bright
polyanthus.*

◀PERENNIALS IN AUTUMN
*The intense autumn foliage
of the grass* Carex oshimensis
'Evergold' *and* Tellima
grandiflora *Rubra Group
is conspicuous in this
adventurous planting.*

The berry theme can be taken up later with winter cherries (*Solanum pseudocapsicum*), just as the vegetable theme can be extended with the showy rosettes of ornamental cabbages. True flowers of autumn and winter are those of heather (*Calluna vulgaris*) and heaths, particularly *Erica carnea* and *E.* × *darleyensis*. These dwarf shrubs mix well with evergreens, including ivies and dwarf trailing conifers. From late winter the palette is brighter, with dwarf bulbs, auriculas, daisies, polyanthus, primroses, and winter-flowering pansies. For trailing plants, in short supply at this season, there is nothing that can match variegated ivies for a crisp effect.

LONG-FLOWERING PLANTS FOR SUMMER

Bidens ferulifolia Tangled stems trailing many small yellow flowerheads.

Convolvulus sabatius Elegantly trailing stems carrying exquisite funnel-shaped flowers from pale to deep lavender-blue.

Diascia vigilis Pretty, bell-shaped flowers in pink on slender stems; other high-performing species and hybrids.

Fuchsia 'Marinka' One of the many trailing fuchsias, producing showers of red flowers.

Impatiens Tempo Series Busy Lizzies in a good colour range.

Lobelia erinus Cascade Series Trailing selection with countless small flowers in shades of pink, red, and blue.

Pelargonium, zonal Numerous choices of erect and bushy pelargoniums flowering non-stop.

Petunia Surfinia Series Among many choices, these are sprawling and have weather-resistant flowers in white, pink, magenta, red, and blue.

Scaevola aemula Stiff-stemmed spreader with many purplish-blue fan-like flowers.

Verbena 'Imagination' Purplish-blue example among many that are trailing or spreading.

GOOD IDEAS FOR HANGING BASKETS

HANGING BASKET ESSENTIALS

THE MATERIALS YOU NEED to make a successful hanging basket are few, inexpensive, and readily available. The simplest container is a plastic-coated wire basket, fitted with chains to suspend it from a strong support. A liner allows excess moisture to drain away but holds in the compost that provides anchorage, nutrients, and water for the plants. The choice of plants is up to you, but trailing and lax plants are naturals for a relaxed look.

A SUCCESSFUL FORMULA
This conventional hanging basket holds bushy and trailing plants for a bright summer display in partial shade.

Three sturdy chains are used to suspend the basket, and to ensure that it is kept on an even keel.

Trailing plants – here yellow begonias and *Lysimachia congestiflora* 'Outback Sunset' – tumble out from the centre.

The bushy *Mimulus* 'Viva' makes an off-centre focus with its numerous boldly splashed flowers.

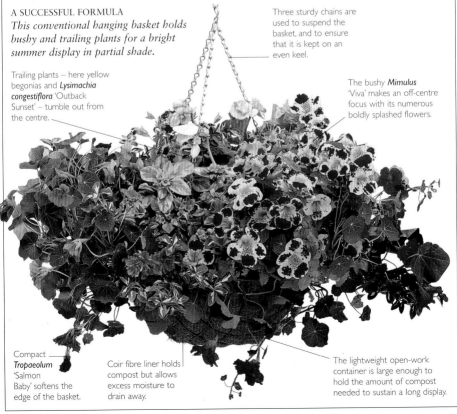

Compact *Tropaeolum* 'Salmon Baby' softens the edge of the basket.

Coir fibre liner holds compost but allows excess moisture to drain away.

The lightweight open-work container is large enough to hold the amount of compost needed to sustain a long display.

◀ TRAILING GLORY *Fuchsias, pelargoniums, and* Helichrysum petiolare *provide a long summer display.*

STANDARD BASKETS

Remember when planting a standard hanging basket that the aim is to create an envelope of loose and trailing stems that will camouflage the container. To get the maximum cascading effect from trailing plants, set them in one or two tiers in the side of the basket, inserting them through slits made in the liner. Above this skirt, plant another level of lax plants around the rim. A bushy plant (or plants) at the centre completes the layered effect.

PLANTING A SUMMER BASKET

Plant baskets in mid-spring so that the displays will have gathered momentum by early summer. Buy young, healthy plants, or use those raised from seed or rooted cuttings (*see pp.53–55*). In frost-prone areas, be sure to keep planted baskets under glass until the danger of frost has passed. Before starting work on the basket, either suspend it from a hook or – more conveniently – stand it level on a bucket or large flowerpot placed in a well-lit position.

YOU NEED:

TOOLS
• Bucket or large flowerpot
• Scissors or craft knife
• Plastic bowl or bucket

MATERIALS
• 35cm (14in) wire hanging basket
• Coir fibre liner
• Potting compost
• Slow-release fertilizer
• Water-retaining granules
• Polythene sheet

PLANTS USED
• Trailing *Lobelia* × 2
• *Helichrysum petiolare* × 2
• Fuchsia × 2
• Ivy-leaved pelargonium × 2
• Surfinia petunia × 2
• *Felicia amelloides* 'Variegata' × 1

LINING THE BASKET

1 Place the basket on a bucket or large flowerpot so that it is centred and level. If the chains or other supports are in the way, detach them. Fit the coir fibre liner, making several cuts, as shown, to ensure a snug fit. With a pre-cut circular liner, simply overlap the segments.

2 Press the coir liner firmly against the bottom and sides of the basket, as it will be when filled with compost. Use scissors to trim off any liner that extends above the rim of the basket, making a neat edge.

Preparing for Planting

1 Using a sharp pair of scissors or a craft knife, make slits about 5cm (2in) long in the side of the liner for planting in tiers. Trailing plants inserted in slits at one or two levels below the surface of the basket will fill out and eventually mask the wire frame.

2 Empty the potting compost into a plastic bowl or bucket and add slow-release fertilizer and water-retaining granules according to the manufacturer's specifications.

3 Add prepared compost to cover the bottom of the basket, filling up to the level of the first tier of slits cut in the side of the liner. Shake down the compost.

4 To protect the trailing plants that are to be inserted through the liner, wrap each in a piece of polythene sheet to form a cone over the stems and leaves.

Planting in Tiers

1 Plant trailing plants – in this case lobelia and *Helichrysum petiolare* – through the slits made in the liner. Working from the inside, thread each plant through, carefully keeping the polythene cone in position to protect the stems and leaves. When the plant is in position, with the root ball on the inside of the liner and the leaves and stems on the outside, gently unwrap and remove the polythene cone.

2 **Continue planting** the bottom tier. Gently tease out the root balls and add compost, working it around the roots and filling to within 5cm (2in) of the rim.

3 **Plant lax plants** – here, fuchsias, pelargoniums, and petunias – around the rim, spaced so that they are not immediately above the plants in the lower tiers.

4 **Add more compost,** working it around the roots and firming gently. Leave a gap in the centre for a bushy plant. *Felicia amelloides* 'Variegata', which is used in this planting, has blue daisy-like flowers and variegated cream-splashed leaves.

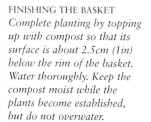

FINISHING THE BASKET
Complete planting by topping up with compost so that its surface is about 2.5cm (1in) below the rim of the basket. Water thoroughly. Keep the compost moist while the plants become established, but do not overwater.

CAGE BASKET FOR SPRING

Plant double daisies and winter-flowering pansies in mid- to late winter for displays that begin reaching their peak in mid-spring. Ivies are useful evergreen trailing plants for early baskets. Hang the basket in a sheltered position outdoors or, in areas with sustained periods of freezing conditions in late winter and spring, display in a conservatory. The birdcage frame of this small, purpose-made hanging basket is 30cm (12in) in diameter.

PLANTING PLAN

1 *Bellis perennis* 'White Carpet' × 4
2 *Ranunculus asiaticus* × 2
3 *Viola* Universal Series × 8
4 *Hedera helix* 'Harald' × 3

MORE CHOICES

Bellis perennis 'Pomponette Pink Buttons' Double daisy with pink flowerheads.
Hedera helix 'Duckfoot' Ivy with three-lobed, glossy green leaves.
Narcissus 'Tête-à-tête' Dwarf daffodil with 1–3 yellow flowers per stem.
Primula Cowichan Blue Group Intense blue polyanthus.
Viola Princess Series Neat, small-flowered pansies.

Ranunculus asiaticus, or Persian buttercup, is a perennial grown as a spring-flowering annual. The double form has numerous delicate petals.

Bellis perennis 'White Carpet' is a double daisy that produces densely packed flowerheads in late winter and spring.

Viola Universal Series are tough winter-flowering pansies with a season that extends well into spring.

Hedera helix 'Harald' is a small-leaved ivy with trailing foliage lit with cream or yellow variegation.

SUMMER BASKET WITH ROSES

Repeat-flowering ground-cover roses are the most suitable of all roses for mixed plantings in containers, and in a sheltered spot in full sun they give a long season throughout the summer. In this harmonious scheme, the lax pale pink rose forms the crown above a full skirt of plants in darker and complementary shades, a pleasing arrangement in which the rose is not overshadowed. Grow in a 45cm (18in) diameter wire hanging basket.

PLANTING PLAN

1 *Rosa* Northamptonshire × 1
2 *Convolvulus sabatius* × 5
3 *Lobelia* 'Lilac Fountain' × 5
4 *Verbena* 'Pink Parfait' × 5

MORE CHOICES

Rosa Avon Compact ground-cover rose; pink buds with pearly white flowers.
Scaevola aemula Stiffly spreading, with purplish fan-like flowers.
Solenopsis axillaris Small starry blue flowers borne in great profusion.
Verbena 'Silver Anne' A verbena not available from seed, with bright pink flowers fading to white.

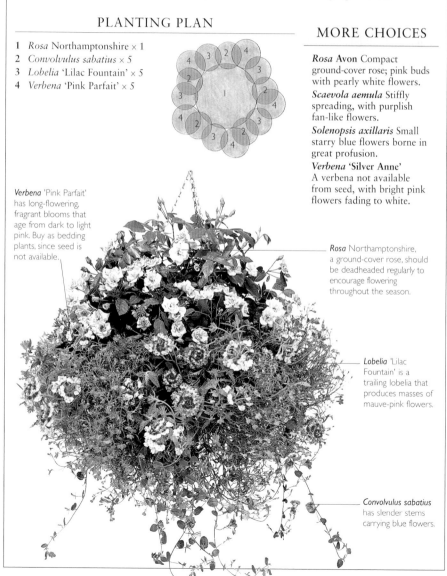

Verbena 'Pink Parfait' has long-flowering, fragrant blooms that age from dark to light pink. Buy as bedding plants, since seed is not available.

Rosa Northamptonshire, a ground-cover rose, should be deadheaded regularly to encourage flowering throughout the season.

Lobelia 'Lilac Fountain' is a trailing lobelia that produces masses of mauve-pink flowers.

Convolvulus sabatius has slender stems carrying blue flowers.

Long-lasting Summer Basket

A basket of sun-loving and long-flowering plants makes a vivid summer display that is skilfully toned down by generous use of foliage. The red flower colour is picked up in the leaves of the coleus, but their yellowish green edge makes a light contrast. The foliage of the ivy-leaved pelargoniums provides a glossy green base, while silvery *Lotus berthelotii* trails with carefree ease. Plant up in a 45cm (18in) diameter wire hanging basket.

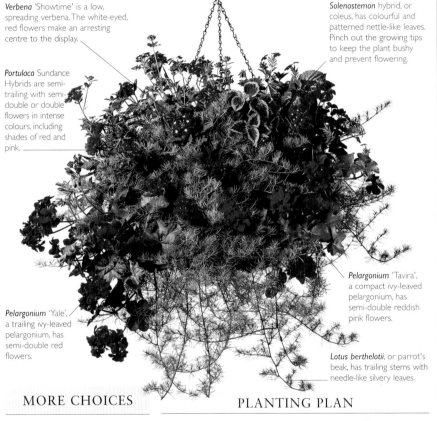

Verbena 'Showtime' is a low, spreading verbena. The white-eyed, red flowers make an arresting centre to the display.

Solenostemon hybrid, or coleus, has colourful and patterned nettle-like leaves. Pinch out the growing tips to keep the plant bushy and prevent flowering.

Portulaca Sundance Hybrids are semi-trailing with semi-double or double flowers in intense colours, including shades of red and pink.

Pelargonium 'Tavira', a compact ivy-leaved pelargonium, has semi-double reddish pink flowers.

Pelargonium 'Yale', a trailing ivy-leaved pelargonium, has semi-double red flowers.

Lotus berthelotii, or parrot's beak, has trailing stems with needle-like silvery leaves.

MORE CHOICES

Pelargonium 'Blazonry' Fancy-leaved zonal with red flowers.
Pelargonium 'Decora Impérial' Ivy-leaved pelargonium with elegant scarlet flowers.
Plecostachys serpyllifolia Grey-leaved trailing foliage plant.
Tropaeolum majus 'Hermine Grashoff' Bright red flowers.

PLANTING PLAN

1 *Solenostemon* hybrid × 2
2 *Verbena* 'Showtime' × 4
3 *Portulaca* Sundance Hybrids × 3
4 *Pelargonium* 'Yale' × 2
5 *Pelargonium* 'Tavira' × 1
6 *Lotus berthelotii* × 4

SUMMER BASKET IN RESTFUL HUES

A restricted palette of yellow and green creates a restrained harmony of hues that suggests radiant sunniness overlying cooler depths. The straying stems of the *Helichrysum petiolare* give the basket its carefree silhouette.

If necessary, check this plant's vigour by pinching back excessive growth from time to time. Remove spent flowers promptly to prolong the cheerful display. Suitable for a 35cm (14in) diameter wire hanging basket.

PLANTING PLAN

1   *Antirrhinum* 'Sweetheart' × 4
2   *Viola* Crystal Bowl Series × 3
3   *Viola* 'Rhine Gold' × 3
4   *Helichrysum petiolare* 'Limelight' × 3
5   *Hedera helix* 'Harald' × 3

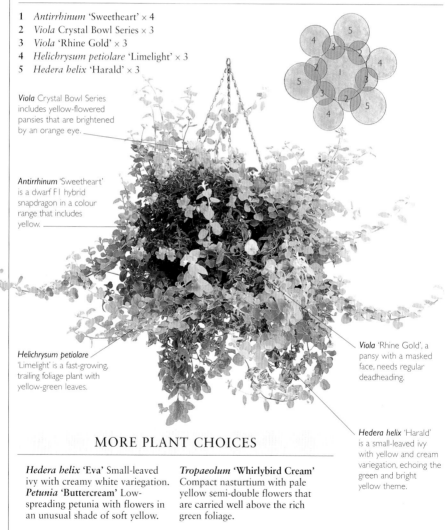

Viola Crystal Bowl Series includes yellow-flowered pansies that are brightened by an orange eye.

Antirrhinum 'Sweetheart' is a dwarf F1 hybrid snapdragon in a colour range that includes yellow.

Helichrysum petiolare 'Limelight' is a fast-growing, trailing foliage plant with yellow-green leaves.

Viola 'Rhine Gold', a pansy with a masked face, needs regular deadheading.

Hedera helix 'Harald' is a small-leaved ivy with yellow and cream variegation, echoing the green and bright yellow theme.

MORE PLANT CHOICES

Hedera helix **'Eva'** Small-leaved ivy with creamy white variegation. *Petunia* **'Buttercream'** Low-spreading petunia with flowers in an unusual shade of soft yellow.

Tropaeolum **'Whirlybird Cream'** Compact nasturtium with pale yellow semi-double flowers that are carried well above the rich green foliage.

SUMMER BASKET IN RICH COLOURS

This mixture of glowing and deep colours would do well in a position that is lightly shaded for part of the day. Deadhead frequently and, as summer advances, cut back pansy stems that become lanky. The new, more compact growth will extend the season by producing a fresh crop of flowers. Grow in a 45cm (18in) diameter wire hanging basket.

Plectranthus madagascariensis 'Variegated Mintleaf' is a reliable houseplant that can also be used to brighten outdoor summer displays.

Mimulus hybrids, or monkey flowers, are moisture-loving plants with snapdragon flowers that are usually speckled or blotched.

Tradescantia zebrina, or wandering Jew, is a trailing perennial that fares well outdoors during summer, although more usually grown as a houseplant.

Viola 'Jolly Joker' is a distinctive summer-flowering pansy with purple and orange markings.

Lobularia maritima 'Wonderland Purple' is a compact dark-flowered form of the scented annual sweet alyssum.

PLANTING PLAN

1 *Mimulus* hybrids × 3
2 *Plectranthus madagascariensis* 'Variegated Mintleaf' × 2
3 *Tradescantia zebrina* × 3
4 *Viola* 'Jolly Joker' × 8
5 *Lobularia maritima* 'Wonderland Purple' × 5

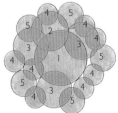

MORE CHOICES

Heliotropium **'Princess Marina'** Heads of fragrant purplish-blue flowers.
Heuchera micrantha **'Palace Purple'** Foliage plant with bronze and jagged leaves; produces small greenish white flowers in summer.
Lantana camara Vigorous-shrub with brick-red and orange flowers.
Solenostemon **hybrid** Dark-leaved coleus.
Verbena **'Peaches and Cream'** Spreading and freely branching with orange-pink flowers fading to cream.

Making a Flower Ball

For this easy but impressive ball shape, densely studded with bloom, you need free-flowering plants of neat growth. Busy Lizzies are ideal and do well in shady positions. Instead of using a commercially produced kit, make your own flower ball using two standard wire baskets and rigid recycled-paper liners. To simplify watering the ball, incorporate a small flowerpot in the top hemisphere that will serve as a reservoir when the ball is watered.

BALL IN FULL BLOOM
Busy Lizzies are compact and produce flat-faced spurred flowers in profusion for months during the summer, which makes them suitable plants for a flower ball.

Impatiens, or busy Lizzies, come in many colours, and several kinds – as in the example shown here – have red-tinted foliage.

You Need:

TOOLS
• Large flowerpot (to support baskets)
• Pencil
• Craft knife
• Pliers

MATERIALS
• Recycled-paper liner × 2
• 30cm (12in) wire hanging basket × 2
• Potting compost
• 9cm (3½in) plastic flowerpot (to act as reservoir)
• Plastic-coated wire
• Chain

Planting Up the First Half

1 Punch out planting holes, spaced about 15cm (6in) apart, in both liners. Fit one liner into a basket.

2 Fill with compost up to the bottom of the holes, then thread plants through from the inside.

3 Add compost, working it around the root balls, then fill to the top. Press lightly to firm the compost.

Making the Reservoir

1 **Turn the second** liner over, place the flowerpot upside down in the centre, and then trace around the pot.

2 **Cut out just inside** the traced circle with a craft knife, then insert the pot, which should fit tightly.

3 **Plant up** the second basket as for the first basket. Water both halves well and allow to drain.

Fixing the Two Halves Together

A small plastic flowerpot inserted at the top makes watering the flower ball an easy task.

Strong chains are required to suspend the ball, which becomes very heavy when watered.

1 **Hinge the baskets** together with short lengths of plastic-coated wire. Now close the baskets together with a quick action. An additional pair of hands is helpful at this stage.

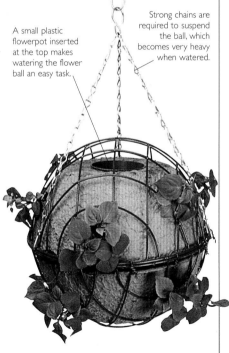

2 **Tie the baskets** together at several evenly spaced points with plastic-coated wire. Use strong chains attached at the junction of the two halves to suspend the finished ball.

HANGING THE BALL
Whether hanging the weighty flower ball temporarily in a well-lit spot under glass or outdoors for summer, make sure it is suspended from a secure support.

MAKING A WOODEN SLATTED BOX

A wooden slatted box makes an attractive and versatile hanging container. Its main use is in the home or conservatory and it is particularly well suited to the growing of orchids, especially those that are pendent or trailing, and specimen ferns. You can buy ready-made boxes, but it is not difficult to make your own using easily obtainable materials and a few tools that are simple to manage.

PRACTICAL TIPS

• To speed up the job, ask your timber supplier to cut the wood into lengths for you.
• Make sure that you use a 10mm (⅜in) bit to drill drainage holes in the plywood base; holes that are too small will result in poor drainage and waterlogged plants.
• When treating the wood, a water-based preservative is preferable; it is less toxic to plants and more pleasant to use than solvent-based products.
• To give the box a long life, reapply water-based preservative every four years or so.

YOU NEED:

TOOLS
• Pencil and tape measure
• Panel saw
• Mitre box
• Electric drill
• 3mm (⅛in) wood bit for holes in side pieces; 10mm (⅜in) wood bit for drainage holes
• Set square
• Pliers
• Paintbrush

MATERIALS
• 14 timber side pieces, each 25×2×2cm (10×¾×¾in)
• 1 plywood base board, 25cm (10in) square
• Strong plastic-coated wire
• Water-based wood preservative
• Polythene sheet
• Potting compost

HOW THE PARTS FIT TOGETHER

THE METHOD
String the base and side pieces on 2 lengths of wire to make a box just over 14cm (5½in) high and with sides 25cm (10in) long. You can also vary the size of the box to suit its intended location.

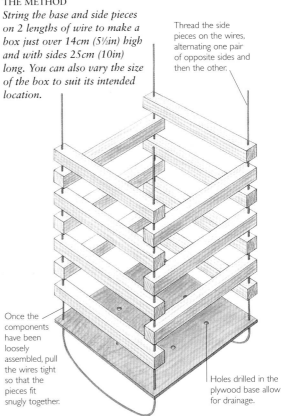

Thread the side pieces on the wires, alternating one pair of opposite sides and then the other.

◄ PLANTING SLATTED BOXES
When used with an appropriate compost, wooden slatted boxes are suitable for growing a wide range of orchids, but they are also attractive containers for many other plants.

Once the components have been loosely assembled, pull the wires tight so that the pieces fit snugly together.

Holes drilled in the plywood base allow for drainage.

CUTTING SIDE PIECES AND PREPARING THE BASE

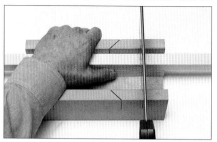 

1 **Measure and mark** the 2x2cm (¾x¾in) timber into 14 side pieces, each 25cm (10in) long. To ensure a straight edge, use a panel saw and mitre box to cut the lengths.

2 **Mark drilling holes** on the same face of each side piece, centred on the width and 1.5cm (½in) in from each end. Drill on an offcut of wood, using a 3mm (⅛in) wood bit.

3 **Use a set square** and pencil to mark out a 25cm (10in) square on the plywood board. Support the board on an offcut of wood while cutting out the shape with a panel saw.

4 **Mark drilling holes** 1.5cm (½in) in from each side at the corners of the plywood square. Rest the plywood on an offcut of wood and drill with a 3mm (⅛in) wood bit.

5 **Mark 7–9** evenly spaced points for drilling drainage holes. Rest the plywood on an offcut of wood and drill through at these points, using a 10mm (⅜in) wood bit.

ASSEMBLING THE SLATTED BOX

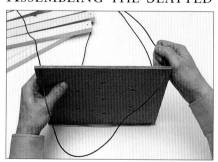 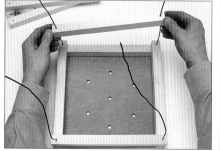

1 **Use pliers to cut** 2 lengths of strong plastic-coated wire, at least 30cm (12in) long. Working from the same side, thread each length of wire through 2 corner holes in the base board, then pull flush with the board.

2 **Make sure there are** four equal lengths of wire above the board, then build up the sides of the box, threading the wires through the holes in the side pieces, alternating one pair of opposite sides and then another.

3 **After threading** through the last pair of side pieces, twist each wire end around a pencil to make a secure loop (*inset*). Cut off excess wire with pliers.

4 **To prolong** the life of the box, paint inside and out with a non-toxic preservative of a suitable colour; or apply marine varnish for a natural wood finish.

THE FINISHED PLANTING

PLANTING PLAN

1 *Blechnum chilense* × 1
2 *Ficus pumila* 'Variegata' × 3

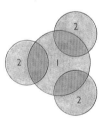

Blechnum chilense is an evergreen fern with dark green fronds.

MORE CHOICES

Davallia canariensis Hare's foot fern, an evergreen fern when grown indoors, has triangular, shiny, mid-green fronds.

Nephrolepis exaltata 'Bostoniensis' Boston fern is evergreen and makes a large, handsome clump of arching fronds.

Platycerium bifurcatum Common staghorn fern, also evergreen, has grey-green fronds that are distinctively branched.

Ficus pumila 'Variegata' is a brightly variegated creeping fig that is also a good trailing plant for indoors.

The box is lined with a sheet of polythene that has holes pierced in the base for drainage.

WALL-MOUNTED BASKETS

NUMEROUS TYPES OF WALL-MOUNTED BASKETS are available in a range of materials, including metal, terracotta, and plastic. Among the largest are those inspired by the traditional stable hayrack made from enamelled or plastic-coated metal. There are also smaller half-baskets and pots, as well as containers to fit in corners. All need to be securely attached to their supports.

PLANTING A HAYRACK

Open-work baskets need to be lined. Use a manufactured liner of the appropriate size or improvise with a sheet of polythene. Straw laid against the outer wall of the basket creates an attractively textured rustic look. A large hayrack allows planting on a generous scale and can successfully take a mixture of culinary herbs and other aromatic plants. To create a cascading effect, make slits in the outer wall of the liner and plant through the grille or mesh of the basket. Either plant up before fixing the hayrack in position or begin with the hayrack securely in place (*see p.59*).

YOU NEED:

MATERIALS
- Hayrack 50cm (20in) long and 24cm (10in) wide
- Straw (for outer liner)
- Polythene sheet (for inner liner)
- Scissors
- Potting compost

LINING THE HAYRACK

1 **For a rustic** look, lay straw against the inner curved face of the hayrack so that when tightly packed it forms a layer about 2.5cm (1in) thick.

2 **Cut a piece** of polythene sheet to make a slightly oversize liner, and fit it inside the hayrack. Fold over the excess towards the straw and tuck in to form a neat edge. Cut slits in the base of the polythene for drainage (*inset*).

◀ HERB BASKET *A generous-sized hayrack is a suitable container for a selection of aromatic herbs.*

PLANTING WITH HERBS AND AROMATIC PLANTS

Fill the hayrack to one-third of its depth with potting compost. Remove plants from their pots, tease out root balls, then arrange the plants in the hayrack. Add or take away compost to get plants to the same level and then top up to within 2.5cm (1in) of the rim and firm the compost. Water well once the hayrack is fixed in position.

PLANTING PLAN

1 *Thymus vulgaris* 'Silver Posie' × 1
2 *Thymus serpyllum* 'Annie Hall' × 1
3 *Pelargonium* 'Lady Plymouth' × 2
4 *Origanum vulgare* 'Aureum' × 2
5 *Salvia officinalis* 'Icterina' × 2
6 *Melissa officinalis* 'Aurea' × 2

Origanum vulgare 'Aureum', or golden wild marjoram, is a spreading shrubby perennial with yellow-green aromatic leaves and pink flowers in summer.

Pelargonium 'Lady Plymouth', a scented-leaved pelargonium, has cut and fingered leaves edged with creamy white.

Melissa officinalis 'Aurea', a variegated lemon balm, is a vigorous perennial with dark green leaves splashed with yellow.

Thymus vulgaris 'Silver Posie', a strongly aromatic shrubby thyme, has frosty variegation and purplish pink flowers.

Salvia officinalis 'Icterina' is a slow-growing sage. Its grey-green leaves have cream margins.

Thymus serpyllum 'Annie Hall' is a low mat-forming thyme with small green leaves and, in early summer, mauve-pink flowers.

MORE PLANT CHOICES FOR HERBS

Allium schoenoprasum Chives have linear tubular leaves with a mild onion flavour and pink flowers in tight heads.

Mentha suaveolens 'Variegata' Pineapple mint is a vigorous plant in moist conditions, with a cool and crisp variegation.

Ocimum basilicum An aromatic annual, basil has bright green leaves; 'Dark Opal' has purple leaves.

Terracotta Wall Pot

Many small wall-mounted containers are made in terracotta, a traditional material for pots, with a colour and texture that is sympathetic to plants. Well-made terracotta wall pots have drainage holes and do not need lining.

For a balanced display, use a low, bushy plant or group of plants for the centre and several trailing plants spilling over the rim to soften the edge. Suitable for a terracotta wall pot 45cm (18in) wide and 33cm (13in) deep.

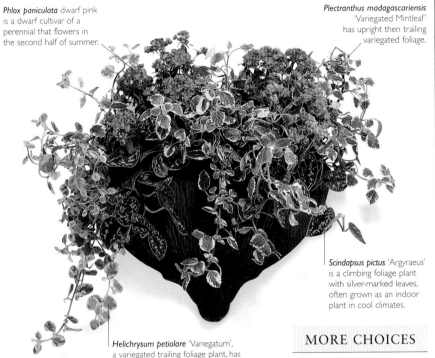

Phlox paniculata dwarf pink is a dwarf cultivar of a perennial that flowers in the second half of summer.

Plectranthus madagascariensis 'Variegated Mintleaf' has upright then trailing variegated foliage.

Scindapsus pictus 'Argyraeus' is a climbing foliage plant with silver-marked leaves, often grown as an indoor plant in cool climates.

Helichrysum petiolare 'Variegatum', a variegated trailing foliage plant, has grey and cream leaves. If necessary, trim back excess growth.

PLANTING PLAN

1 *Plectranthus madagascariensis* 'Variegated Mintleaf' × 3
2 *Phlox paniculata* dwarf pink × 2
3 *Scindapsus pictus* 'Argyraeus' × 2
4 *Helichrysum petiolare* 'Variegatum' × 1

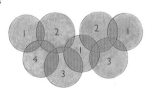

MORE CHOICES

Glechoma hederacea **'Variegata'** Trailing variegated ground ivy.

Impatiens **New Guinea hybrids** Free-flowering busy Lizzies in strong colours; foliage is beautifully marked.

Lobularia maritima **'Little Dorrit'** Loosely spreading; small, scented white flowers.

Lysimachia nummularia **'Aurea'** Creeping evergreen.

Mimulus **hybrids** Flowers freely in partial shade.

IMPROVISED CONTAINERS

MANY HOUSEHOLD ITEMS and other containers have the potential to make hanging baskets of distinctive character. When using containers that have an openwork structure, such as wicker baskets, add a polythene liner. Other containers, such as old buckets, do not not need a liner but must have holes drilled in the base to allow adequate drainage. Before filling containers with compost and plants, fix cords or chain that will provide a secure support.

WICKER BASKET

Both old and new wicker baskets make attractively textured containers and they come in a wide range of sizes, shapes, and woven patterns. If treated with a preservative, a basket can be used outdoors for several years. The robust structure of wicker baskets allows for the planting style to be varied; for example, some or all of the plants can be kept in their original pots.

PRACTICAL TIPS

• Choose a sturdily made basket.
• Use small baskets for single plants.
• For mixed plantings, choose a medium-sized basket that will take the extra weight.
• Strong cord is a more sympathetic material than metal chain for suspending the basket; space three lengths evenly around the rim.
• Empty baskets at the end of season, clean, and reapply the preservative.

YOU NEED:

TOOLS
• Large flowerpot or bucket
• Paintbrush
• Scissors

MATERIALS
• Wicker basket 35cm (14in) in diameter and 15cm (6in) deep
• Coloured water-based wood preservative
• Polythene sheet
• Potting compost
• Strong cord

PAINTING THE BASKET

1 **To protect the** basket, paint it inside and out with a coloured water-based wood preservative, as here, or with a clear marine varnish. Allow the basket to dry thoroughly before lining and filling it with compost.

WOOD PRESERVATIVE
Coloured water-based wood preservatives come in a range of colours, from deep blue to soft lilac and silvery green. They are harmless to plants, water repellent, and combat surface algae.

BLUE-GREY   LAVENDER   GREY-GREEN

◀NATURAL LOOK Convolvulus sabatius *trails from a wicker basket filled with pelargoniums.*

LINING THE BASKET

Place the basket on a large flowerpot or bucket. Lay a sheet of polythene in the basket, pushing it down so that it fully covers the bottom, and cut around the rim to make a slightly oversized liner. Cut a few slits about 5cm (2in) long in the bottom for drainage. Fill the basket a quarter full with potting compost and then trim off excess liner to just below the rim of the basket.

PLANTING UP

1 **Position three miniature** roses in their terracotta pots so that these are almost touching in the centre of the basket. If necessary, scrape compost to the sides so that the pots are all at the same depth and almost sitting on the bottom. Half-fill the basket with compost, working it around the pots, ensuring that they are level and stable.

2 **Remove the ivies** from their pots and arrange them around the edge of the container so that they trail over. If several plants are growing together in a pot, gently break up and use individual plants to fill in small gaps where possible. Top up with compost to a level about 2.5cm (1in) below the rim of the basket, and firm gently.

FINISHED BASKET

Using the strong, thin cord that has been attached to the basket, hang it in a position that is sheltered and sunny for most of the day. Water thoroughly. During the summer keep well watered and apply a liquid feed (*see p.60*) approximately every 10 days.

Deadhead the miniature roses regularly to encourage further flowering, and trim off any unwanted ivy stems. To re-use roses in displays the following summer, repot them between autumn and late winter and trim lightly.

PLANTING PLAN

1 Miniature red rose in terracotta pot × 3
2 *Hedera helix* Yellow variegated × 2
3 *Hedera helix* White variegated × 2

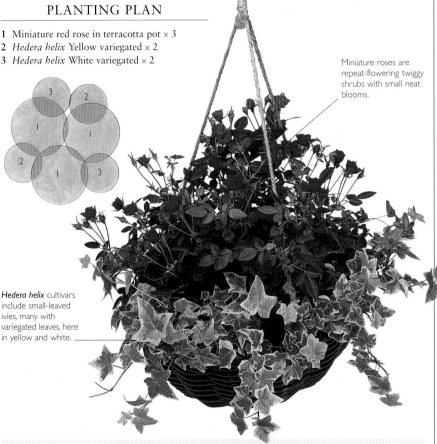

Miniature roses are repeat-flowering twiggy shrubs with small neat blooms.

Hedera helix cultivars include small-leaved ivies, many with variegated leaves, here in yellow and white.

MORE POTTED PLANT CHOICES

Capsicum annuum Longum Group Curved and pointed chilli peppers, turning red in summer.
Hyacinthus Hyacinths with candle-like spires of waxy fragrant flowers in spring.

Lilium **'Red Carpet'** In summer, rich red flowers on plants 30cm (12in) high.
Pelargonium **Regal hybrids** Large-flowered pelargoniums giving a showy display in a sheltered site in summer.

Pericallis × *hybrida* Cinerarias with long-lasting heads of colourful daisies in spring, some bicoloured.
Primula auricula Flowers in unusual colours, often with mealy centres, in spring.

ORNAMENTAL WIRE BASKET

You can make a hanging container from an ornamental wire basket by attaching chains for its support. For a textured effect, line with hessian so that the material overlaps at the top by about 5cm (2in). Turn down the excess on the inside and hold in place with clothes pegs until the basket is filled. Lay a sheet of polythene cut to size inside the hessian, making slits in the bottom for drainage. Do not trim it until the basket is filled with compost.

YOU NEED:

TOOLS
• Scissors
• 3 or 4 clothes pegs
• Pliers (to attach chain)

MATERIALS
• Ornamental wire basket 30cm (12in) wide and 12cm (5in) deep
• Hessian (for outer liner)
• Polythene sheet (for inner liner)
• Potting compost
• Chain

PLANTING PLAN

1 *Ranunculus asiaticus* × 3
2 Polyanthus × 2
3 *Primula vulgaris* × 2
4 *Hedera helix* cultivar × 4
  Any small-leaved, prettily variegated kind

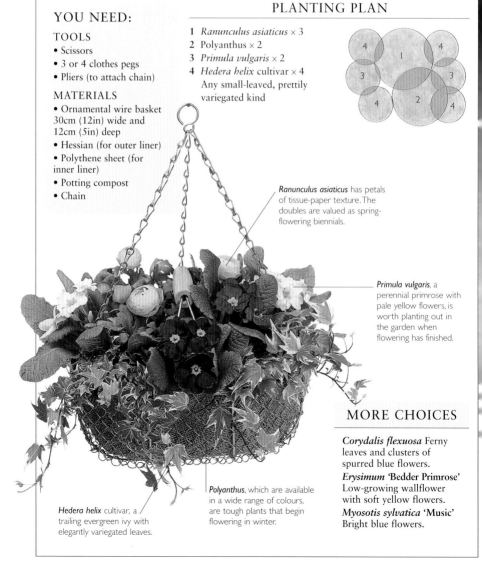

Ranunculus asiaticus has petals of tissue-paper texture. The doubles are valued as spring-flowering biennials.

Primula vulgaris, a perennial primrose with pale yellow flowers, is worth planting out in the garden when flowering has finished.

Hedera helix cultivar; a trailing evergreen ivy with elegantly variegated leaves.

Polyanthus, which are available in a wide range of colours, are tough plants that begin flowering in winter.

MORE CHOICES

Corydalis flexuosa Ferny leaves and clusters of spurred blue flowers.
Erysimum 'Bedder Primrose' Low-growing wallflower with soft yellow flowers.
Myosotis sylvatica 'Music' Bright blue flowers.

Ivy in an Egg Basket

The chicken shape of this egg basket provides an armature on which to train the stems of a small-leaved ivy. Line the basket to about half its depth with hessian, and then with a sheet of polythene (*see facing page*). Add potting compost and plant three small-leaved ivies of the same kind. Pull the stems through the wire and then train over the head and tail and around the base. For a tight topiary shape, tie in growths and shorten long stems.

YOU NEED:
• Egg basket, "body" approximately 23cm (9in) wide and 12cm (5in) deep
• Scissors
• Hessian (for outer liner)
• 3 or 4 clothes pegs
• Polythene sheet (for inner liner)
• Potting compost
• Chain

Use a single chain and hook arrangement to suspend the basket.

Keep the handles of the basket free of plants so that the simple outline is not obscured.

To keep the head well defined, tie in stems and shorten growths.

An outer lining of hessian has a pleasing colour and texture that complements both basket and plants.

MORE SMALL-LEAVED IVY CHOICES

PLAIN-LEAVED	CREAM AND YELLOW VARIEGATED	WHITE AND GREY VARIEGATED
'Asterisk'	'Adam'	'Bruder Ingobert'
'Duckfoot'	'Ambrosia'	'Glacier'
'Midget'	'Eva'	'Kolibri'
'Pin Oak'	'Goldchild'	'Little Diamond'
'Triton'		'White Knight'

METAL TROUGH

Shallow galvanized metal buckets, troughs, large bread tins, and similar items make innovative hanging containers. The metal will not rust, although the surface dulls over time; but whether shiny or matt, the metal colour goes well with bluish foliage, as in the juniper used here for an autumn and winter display, or silver schemes using plants such as those suggested in Plant Choices for a Summer Silver Theme (*see facing page*).

YOU NEED:

TOOLS
- Masking tape
- Electric drill; 3mm (⅛in) metal bit; 10mm (⅜in) metal bit
- Pencil • Pliers (to attach chain)

MATERIALS
- Galvanized metal trough 30cm (12in) long and 14cm (5½in) deep
- Strong plastic-coated wire
- Chain
- Broken crocks (for drainage)
- Potting compost

DRILLING DRAINAGE HOLES

1 **Place masking tape** at the positions of the drainage holes to stop the bit from slipping. Raise the trough on bricks at either side so that there is room to drill through.

2 **It is easiest** to make an initial hole using a small 3mm (⅛in) bit, then enlarge it using a 10mm (⅜in) bit. Steady the bit on the tape and drill through.

THREADING WIRE AND MAKING EYELETS

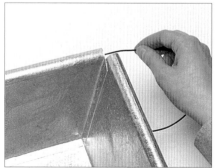 

1 **To provide points** of attachment for the chains to suspend the trough, thread a generous length of strong plastic-coated wire through the hollow rim formed by the rolled metal edge.

2 **To form eyelets**, make a small loop at each corner of the trough as you thread the wire through. Insert a pencil in the loop and then turn several times. Attach the chains to the eyelets.

PLANTING THE TROUGH

Place a layer of drainage material, such as broken crocks, in the base of the trough; half-fill with compost. Remove each plant from its pot before setting it in place.

Arrange the euonymus and juniper side by side in the centre, then tuck the ivies around the edge. Add more compost between the plants while gently firming them in place.

PLANTING PLAN

1 *Euonymus fortunei* 'Emerald Gaiety' × 1
2 *Juniperus horizontalis* 'Blue Chip' × 1
3 *Hedera helix* Any small-leaved cultivars × 4

Euonymus fortunei 'Emerald Gaiety' is a compact evergreen shrub with bright green leaves edged in white; in winter, the variegation flushes pink.

Juniperus horizontalis 'Blue Chip' is a compact, prostrate evergreen conifer with prickly blue-green foliage.

Hedera helix cultivar, a small-leaved and variegated trailing ivy.

PLANT CHOICES FOR A SUMMER SILVER THEME

Argyranthemum 'Snow Storm' Compact white daisy with grey-green leaves.
Helichrysum petiolare Vigorous trailing foliage plant.
Lotus berthelotii Trailing plant with silver-green leaves.

Pelargonium 'Flower of Spring' Fancy-leaved zonal pelargonium with variegated leaves and scarlet flowers.
P. 'L'Elégante' White variegated ivy-leaved pelargonium with white flowers.

Plecostachys serpyllifolia Trailing, with small grey leaves.
Plectranthus madagascariensis 'Variegated Mintleaf' White variegated foliage plant.
Senecio cineraria 'Silver Dust' Upright silver foliage plant.

MATERIALS AND ROUTINE CARE

RAISING HANGING BASKET PLANTS

GROWING PLANTS FROM SEED is itself an enjoyable part of gardening, and filling hanging baskets with plants you have raised yourself is satisfying, and generally much cheaper than using stock bought from nurseries and garden centres. Annuals – plants that squeeze their whole life cycle into a single growing season – are particularly rewarding and most, including half-hardy annuals, are easy to raise from seed.

GROWING FROM SEED

Half-hardy annuals, a category including several short-lived perennials such as petunias, are unable to withstand frost. They are usually sown in containers so that in their early stages, plants can be kept in a protected environment. Use fresh seed compost and sow thinly in a clean tray or pot. For best results, place the container in an electrically heated propagator, if you have one, maintaining a temperature of 13–21°C (55–70°F). Good results are possible even on a kitchen windowsill. Seed packets specify particular temperature and light requirements.

1 Fill a clean tray with seed compost and firm to a level surface 1.5cm (½in) below the rim. Water with a fine rose and leave for an hour to drain thoroughly. Sow the seeds thinly and evenly, gently tapping them from the seed packet or a fold of paper.

2 Leave dust-like seeds uncovered, but cover larger seeds with a fine layer of sieved compost. Water lightly, by standing the tray in water if the seeds are small. Cover the tray with a sheet of glass or plastic to maintain even humidity. Shade lightly until seed germinates.

◄ EASY ACCESS *A pulley arrangement allows hanging baskets to be lowered for watering* (see p.60).

Pricking Out

If left crowded together in a seed tray, seedlings become weak and spindly. Pricking out is the procedure of moving them on to compartmented trays or pots where they can develop before they are ready to be planted outdoors. To minimize any check to growth, handle carefully when transferring seedlings to new containers. Damaged roots and leaves are entry points for disease, which can quickly prove fatal. For a few days, maintain humidity by placing the container under a see-through plastic cover kept clear of the plants. Keep in a light place away from direct sunlight.

PLANTS TO GROW FROM SEED

All the following are or can be grown as half-hardy annuals

Busy Lizzy *Impatiens walleriana.*
Marigold Low-growing *Tagetes* hybrids.
Lobelia Compact and trailing cultivars of *Lobelia erinus.*
Monkey flower Showy *Mimulus* hybrids.
Nasturtium Semi-trailing selections of *Tropaeolum majus,* such as the Gleam Series.
Pelargonium F1 and F2 seed selections.
Petunia Most *Petunia* hybrids.
Verbena Many *Verbena* hybrids.

1 Give the tray a sharp knock to loosen the soil. Use a clean widger or a pencil to separate seedlings and when lifting, hold by the small seed leaves, which are the first leaves to appear.

2 Make a hole in the compost and transplant the seedling, retaining as much compost as possible around the roots. Insert the seedling, gently firm the compost around it, and then water, using a fine rose.

HARDENING OFF

Acclimatizing plants to conditions outdoors is known as hardening off. A closed frame makes a useful halfway house. The ventilation is increased over several weeks by gradually raising the frame light, a little more each day, and closing it at night. When the risk of frost has passed, the frame light is removed completely. To harden off without a frame, place young plants in a sheltered position outdoors during the day. Cover at night or in severe weather during the day, using a sheet of clear plastic or fleece on a temporary wire or bamboo frame. Dispense with the cover once all danger of night frosts has passed.

HARDENING OFF SEEDLINGS IN A COLD FRAME

BUYING PLANTS

- Starting with healthy vigorous plants is the best guarantee of a successful hanging basket.
- Buying plants saves time, you can select plants according to their quality, and you can choose according to colour (seed is often available only in mixtures).
- Half-hardy bedding plants are the main purchases for containers. These may be sold as seedlings or seedling plugs (*see right*) or as more advanced plants, including mature specimens in full flower.

- Young plants sold in spring often have not been hardened off, and are not suitable for immediate planting outside.
- Look for sturdy, compact plants with healthy foliage. The root system should be well developed, but avoid pot-bound plants.
- Avoid plants with lanky growth, yellowing foliage, signs of pests, and any that are in dried-out pots.

SEEDLING PLUG

TAKING A CUTTING

Many shrubby perennials and true shrubs, among them fuchsias and pelargoniums, are easily raised from cuttings. When grown in containers, these plants are often discarded at the end of summer but cuttings from them can become the next generation of vigorous free-flowering plants. Take cuttings in late summer or early autumn, and overwinter under glass to give well-developed plants for early summer. Alternatively, overwinter the parent plant and take cuttings in spring. Minimize the risk of disease by using fresh compost, clean pots, and a clean blade. It is not always possible to find a non-flowering shoot from which to take a cutting; in such cases, remove flowers and buds after taking the cutting.

1 **Detach a healthy** non-flowering shoot (here of a pelargonium) 8–15cm (3–6in) long, making the cut just below a node – a joint on the stem where natural growth hormones are most active and leaves develop.

2 **Using a sharp knife,** remove all but the top two leaves and, if the plant has large leaves, trim these by half.

3 **Trim the base** of the cutting straight across just below the bottom joint. Dip the cut end in a hormone rooting powder.

4 **Insert the cutting** in a pot filled with moist compost. Insert other cuttings, not touching, around the edge and firm well.

CONTAINERS, LINERS, AND COMPOSTS

THE RAW MATERIALS OF A HANGING BASKET are functional rather than decorative. Nonetheless, commercially produced baskets and liners come in a range of designs in various materials, and there is a choice of composts, including relatively light soilless kinds and heavier formulations that are soil based.

CHOOSING CONTAINERS

When buying hanging and wall-mounted containers, check for sturdy construction, paying particular attention to the method of attachment. Most plastic-coated wire or enamelled aluminium containers will give service for many years. Dark colours have the advantage of blending with foliage, quickly becoming inconspicuous as plants start to grow away. Good drainage is essential in all containers.

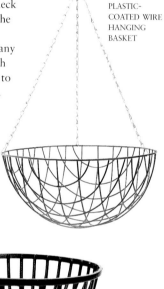

PLASTIC-COATED WIRE HANGING BASKET

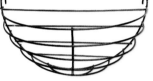

HAYRACK-STYLE WALL BASKET

TERRACOTTA WALL POT

EGG BASKET AS AN IMPROVISED CONTAINER

ENAMELLED ALUMINIUM HANGING BASKET

HANGING POTS

The suspended pot, usually in plastic, is an alternative to the hanging basket. It often comes complete with a clip-on tray to hold water. Hanging pots are planted from the top, so they are less fiddly to plant up than a conventional basket. A disadvantage is that their solid construction prevents planting in the sides; they are generally seen to best effect if hung low so that the view is onto the plants, not up to the pot. Self-watering pots contain a reservoir with a wick in the form of capillary matting, which keeps the compost moist. This reduces the need for frequent watering.

SELF-WATERING PLASTIC POT

LINERS FOR HANGING BASKETS

Commercially produced liners in various sizes are made from a wide range of materials. Some liners are flexible, such as those made of coir fibre, wool, and foam plastic. Those made from recycled paper are rigid. Polythene sheet is a versatile and inexpensive liner, easily cut to size and slit to allow drainage. It can be combined with an attractive outer lining of, say, hessian or straw (*see below*). The texture and colour of the liner matters when there is no thick skirt of plants to hide the basket.

SPHAGNUM MOSS

A number of mosses growing in boggy conditions are sold as sphagnum moss – the traditional material for lining hanging baskets. It has remarkable moisture-holding properties and, because of its natural colour and texture, it makes a sympathetic base for plants. Its large-scale collection from the wild is, however, a cause for environmental concern and it does not lend itself to cultivation. Although it remains available, the use of substitutes is now strongly recommended.

COIR FIBRE
Rough-textured pads, laid with overlapping segments. Natural-looking, but tricky to cut for side planting.

FOAM
Mottled pads of foam plastic, pre-cut into segments. Absorb moisture well, easy to cut, but conspicuous.

RECYCLED PAPER
Rigid cardboard liners. Cheap; can be difficult to cut, but most have push-out holes in the sides for planting.

WOOL
Soft-textured and mottled circular pads. Difficult to cut, but insulating properties protect plants' roots.

OUTER LINERS

An outer liner of a well-textured material that is sympathetic to plants can be used to hide an unglamorous, practical inner liner cut to size from polythene. Use a double lining when the skirt of trailing plants will be flimsy, as is often the case with spring displays. Hessian takes up little room and has a good texture and colour. Straw is bulky, but appropriate in rustic-style containers such as hayracks.

HESSIAN

STRAW

COMPOSTS

• The compost for a hanging basket must give good anchorage and hold the moisture and nutrients necessary for vigorous plant growth. There are several proprietary composts available that fulfil these needs.

• Soilless composts are ideal for hanging baskets as they are light and easy to handle. Many have been based on peat, but for environmental reasons it is preferable to use soilless composts based on peat substitutes, such as coir fibre. These are readily available as general-purpose composts.

• Soil-based potting composts, which are heavier than soilless composts, are suitable for shrubby plants such as roses. The formula John Innes No. 2 suits most plants.

• Some plants, such as heathers, dislike lime. Grow them in an ericaceous compost, which is lime-free and acidic.

METHODS OF FIXING AND HANGING

Hanging baskets and wall-mounted containers may look light and airy, but when filled with moist compost and plants they are heavy items. The collapse of a container not merely risks spoiling a display. It can also cause damage and be a real danger to people. Ensure that all supports are sturdy, make all fixings secure, and check connections of closed-link chains or cords before hanging filled containers. Check all equipment and fittings annually before rehanging baskets.

FIXING A WALL BRACKET

Most wall brackets for hanging baskets are made of cast aluminium or wrought iron, sometimes plastic coated. Designs differ but the consistent features are a back plate and a braced arm, from the end of which the basket is suspended. The arm needs to be long enough for the basket to hang clear of the vertical wall to which the back plate is attached. Brackets come in a range of sizes, so make sure that you have the correct size for the diameter of basket you plan to use. Fixing is by screws through the back plate and into the wall. Use wall plugs if fixing into a masonry wall. Mount the bracket in a sheltered position where the basket will hang without being in the way.

TIPS FOR OTHER FIXTURES

• Hanging baskets suspended from overhead supports need a strong fixing. Indoors, use stout swivel hooks to screw into ceiling joists.

• The same sort of fixing can be used for hanging baskets suspended from the beams of a pergola. The alternative is to attach the basket with cords lashed over the beams.

• Hang baskets so that they are not in the way of pedestrian traffic. Pergolas often provide positions in light shade for part of the day, which suit many mixtures of plants.

• Lashing with cords is the best way of attaching baskets to the branches of trees; however, remember that the conditions may suit only shade-tolerant plants.

1 Mark the positions of the holes, then use an electric drill with a masonry bit to drill out holes large enough to take a screw and wall plug.

2 To provide a sound fixing for the screws, set a wall plug matching the size of the screw and of suitable length in each hole and knock it in with a hammer.

3 Place the bracket against the wall with the back plate holes over the wall plugs. Insert a galvanized or brass screw in each hole and fix securely in place.

FIXING A HAYRACK TO A WALL

Wall-mounted containers are fixed in position in various ways. The hayrack below has brackets that are fitted to the wall from which the container is hung. Many smaller containers are simply screwed directly to a surface or have holes in the back plate that allow the container to be hung from screws standing proud of the wall. One of the simplest types of wall-mounted container is a wire bracket hung vertically to hold a plain pot. Use wall plugs when fixing screws into masonry.

1 Hold the container against the wall and mark its approximate position, ruling a line across the top with a wax crayon or chalk. Check this line with a spirit level and adjust if necessary. Hold the container up again and mark the position of the brackets.

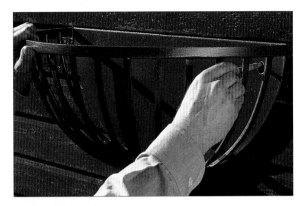

2 Place the right-hand bracket in position and mark the holes for the screws that will support it. Using an electric drill and a wood or masonry bit, drill the holes (*inset*), then fix the bracket in position with galvanized screws. Do the same for the left-hand bracket. If drilling into masonry, insert wall plugs.

3 Lift the hayrack into position and set it on the brackets. The container can be taken down to plant up. Alternatively, because of its weight when full, it can be lined and filled with plants in its mounted position.

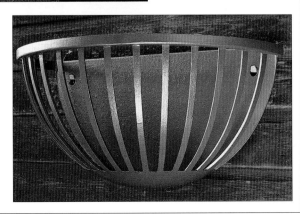

Maintaining Plants

Hanging baskets give a return out of all proportion to the labour involved in planting and maintaining them. The intimate care of plants can in itself give great pleasure. Many gardeners enjoy enormously the day-to-day business of watering and grooming their small containerized gardens. But it is possible, using modern fertilizers and watering equipment, to have truly splendid hanging baskets without being tied to routine care.

Watering Effectively

Planted containers need frequent watering; relying on rainfall (at best an irregular supply) is rarely enough. Positions near walls are usually in rainshadow, and foliage tends to shed water outside containers. Water by hand or with an irrigation system, directing water near the base of plants. Water more often in sunny and windy weather. Water-retaining granules or gel added to the compost will help to slow down water loss.

▲ RISE-AND-FALL PULLEY FITTING
A pulley attachment (inset) that allows a hanging basket to be raised, lowered, and held in a locked position simplifies watering and grooming.

▲ HOSE LANCE ATTACHMENT
A lance attachment with trigger-action is a useful extension to a hose. Alternatively, use a simple hose with its end tied to a length of cane.

FEEDING PLANTS

• The dense planting of a hanging basket makes heavy demands on the nutrients in a relatively small quantity of compost.

• To keep plants healthy and vigorous, add slow-release inorganic fertilizers, sold as granules, tablets, or pellets, to the compost before planting. These release nutrients gradually throughout the growing season.

• Alternatively, boost nutrient levels by applying soluble inorganic fertilizers on a regular basis according to the instructions.

DRIP-FEED IRRIGATION SYSTEMS

You can create a simple drip-feed irrigation system from components readily available at garden centres and DIY stores. First check local and national regulations. There is a general requirement that a tap with hose must be fitted with a double-check valve. Use micro-tubing fitted with a fixed-output or adjustable dripper to carry water from a supply pipe to individual containers. The system can be automated, delivering water for a certain period at set intervals.

SECTION OF SYSTEM

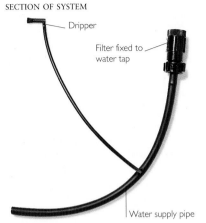

Dripper

Filter fixed to water tap

Water supply pipe

ADJUSTABLE DRIPPER

FIXED-OUTPUT DRIPPER

GROOMING

In a well-balanced mixture, the plants in a hanging basket interweave and knit together with very little help from the gardener. To encourage good overall development, rotate the basket regularly, giving plants even exposure to light. Some plants, such as the scented-leaved pelargoniums, may need pinching back to encourage bushy or spreading growth. Others, like the trailing *Helichrysum petiolare*, may need pinching back to check excessive growth. Remove dead leaves or untidy stems. To keep plants flowering over a long season, remove spent flowers promptly. Once plants begin to set seed, they stop putting energy into producing flowers.

DEADHEADING
Remove spent flowers promptly to maintain a long-lasting display. Simply pinch off faded blooms between fingers and thumb; for tougher stems, use a pair of scissors.

AVOIDING PROBLEMS

• Serious problems are unlikely if you take sensible precautions.
• Start with healthy, vigorous plants and grow them in fresh compost.
• Place containers in positions that suit the plants you are growing.
• Water frequently and ensure that plants are well fed.
• Remove any dead or diseased growth as soon as you notice it.
• Keep an eye open for pests and deal with them promptly. The most likely to cause trouble are greenfly and blackfly, which are both sap-sucking aphids. Various controls are available, some synthetic, others organic. Apply all controls according to the manufacturer's instructions.

GOOD PLANTS FOR BASKETS

THE FOLLOWING SELECTIONS cover flowering and foliage plants for outdoor hanging baskets and wall-mounted containers, edible plants, which are mainly culinary herbs, and flowering and foliage plants for the house or conservatory. Where the climate is mild enough, many of the indoor plants can be moved outdoors during the summer months. Use bushy and upright plants in the centre of the basket to make a domed crown, and rely on spreading, lax, and trailing plants at the edge and sides to complete a pleasing outline.

◳ *Prefers full sun* ◳ *Tolerates full sun or partial shade* ◳ *Prefers partial shade* ✳ *Tolerates full shade* ✴✴✴ *Fully hardy* ✴✴ *Frost hardy* ✴ *Half hardy* ◔ *Frost tender* ♀ *RHS Award of Garden Merit*

FLOWERING PLANTS

THE EMPHASIS IN THIS SELECTION is on flowering plants that are colourful during a long period in summer. In many cases the entries include recommended cultivars, sometimes of mixtures that offer a wide colour range. When making a choice, take into account flower texture, shape, size, and colour, and consider also whether plants are erect or more lax in growth.

Ageratum
(Floss flower)
Compact long-flowering annual for the centre of the basket. In summer fluffy clustered flowerheads, mainly in shades of blue, but also white and pink, stand just above the mound of foliage. Good blues include 'Adriatic' and 'Blue Danube'.
◳ ✴

Argyranthemum
(Marguerite)
Shrubby and long-flowering daisies, some double, making

BEGONIA NONSTOP SERIES ♀

cheerful summer displays in containers. Two compact hybrids with grey-green foliage and yellow-centred daisies that are suitable for the centre of a basket are 'Petite Pink' ♀, a light pink, and 'Snow Storm' ♀, with white florets.
◳ ✴

Begonia, upright hybrids
(Tuberhybrida begonia)
In summer upright plants with succulent stems carry double rose-like flowers, often very vivid, over glossy leaves. Some hybrids have ruffled petals

◀ FULL BLOOM *A classic summer hanging basket, including fuchsias, petunias, and verbenas.*

and some have contrasting petal tips. The colours in the Nonstop Series ♀ are strong and clear. Start tubers into growth in spring and plant in the centre of the basket.
🔲 ❧

Begonia, pendulous hybrids
(Pendula begonia)
Planting in a suspended container shows off flowers clustered on trailing stems below glossy leaves. Start tubers into growth in spring and plant at the edge of baskets for a trailing display in summer. The Cascade Series and the Sensation Series are doubles in a wide colour range.
🔲 ❧

Bellis perennis
(Common daisy)
Plant the double forms at the edge of spring baskets. The flowerheads that rise from a tuft of spoon-shaped leaves are densely packed with florets, white or shades of pink and red around a yellow centre. 'Pomponette' ♀ has neat button flowerheads.
🔲 ✳✳✳

CONVOLVULUS SABATIUS

Bidens ferulifolia ♀
A tangle of slender stems supports a constellation of starry yellow daisy flowerheads from summer to autumn. Grow as an annual and plant at the edge of containers. Trim excess growth if necessary.
🔲 ✳✳

Calluna vulgaris
(Heather, Ling)
Low evergreen shrub, which must have an ericaceous or lime-free compost. The flower spikes are borne from late summer on, and the numerous cultivars are useful at the edge or centre of autumn and winter displays. Most have flowers in shades of pink and purple, but 'Anthony Davis' ♀ and 'White Lawn' ♀ are among those with white flowers, and 'Darkness' ♀ is a good crimson. The foliage, often bronzed or yellow, can be attractive when plants are not in flower.
🔲 ✳✳✳

Convolvulus sabatius ♀
Slender perennial with whimsical trailing stems carrying numerous funnel-shaped flowers of refined beauty in summer and early autumn. The colour range extends from soft mauve-blue to rich blue. Plant in the sides and at the edge of baskets.
🔲 ✳✳

Diascia
The prostrate stems of several perennial species and hybrids trail, and the sprays of small spurred flowers, in shades of pink, make an airy decoration throughout summer when planted at the edge of containers. *D. rigescens* ♀, with deep pink flowers, trails

BIDENS FERULIFOLIA ♀

stiffly. The creeping *D. vigilis* ♀, softer in effect, has clear pink flowers. The numerous pink-flowered hybrids include 'Lilac Belle' ♀, a soft mauve, and 'Ruby Field', which is salmon pink.
🔲 ✳✳

Dorotheanthus bellidiformis
(Livingstone daisy, Mesembryanthemum)
In sun, the daisy flowers are dazzling and almost hide the fleshy leaves, but in dull weather they close. This low annual, raised from seed, provides a wide colour range for summer, from yellow to red, often with a white throat. 'Lunette' is soft yellow with a red centre. Plant at the edge or sides of baskets.
🔲 ✳

Erica carnea
(Heath, Heather)
Dwarf and tough evergreen shrub flowering in winter and spring, providing colour at a low point in the year. Of the many cultivars, most have purple-pink flowers. 'Challenger' ♀ is strong magenta, 'Myretoun Ruby' ♀

is pink changing to crimson, and 'Springwood White' ♀ is a clean white. Plant at the centre or edge of the basket. ☐ ❋❋❋

Felicia amelloides
(Blue daisy)
Sun-loving shrubby daisy, often grown as an annual, with numerous bright blue yellow-centred flowerheads right through summer and into autumn. The rounded bushes tend to be large for hanging baskets, but 'Read's Blue' and 'Read's White' are compact and suitable for a central position.
☐ ◈

Fuchsia
The elegant flowers, produced freely throughout summer, and the lax trailing growth of many fuchsias make them outstanding among shrubby plants for containers. There are also compact upright cultivars suitable for the centre of a basket. The flowers, single or double and often bicoloured, are in shades of pink, purple, and red, or white. Good examples of

FUCHSIA 'JACK SHAHAN'

FELICIA AMELLOIDES
'READ'S WHITE'

trailing kinds include 'Auntie Jinks', a single with white and purple flowers; 'Jack Shahan' ♀, single and rich pink; 'La Campanella' ♀, small semi-double that is white and purple, and 'Marinka' ♀, single and strong red. Upright kinds include 'Annabel' ♀, with white double flowers flushed pink, and 'Tom Thumb' ♀, a single with many small flowers in red and purple.
☐ ❋❋ to ◈

Gazania
In summer, large, jaunty flowerheads, mainly in shades of yellow, bronze, pink, and red, often with boldly contrasted zones, stand above clumps of grey-backed leaves. Plant at the edge or centre in full sun; the flowers close in poor light. The Chansonette and Daybreak Series offer a good range of warm colours.
☐ ❋

Impatiens
(Busy Lizzie)
The compact and spreading cultivars of I. walleriana bear flat-faced and semi-double or

double spurred flowers over a long summer season. They are versatile plants for the sides, edge, or centre of the basket. Some are of startling brilliance, but there are also softer tones of pink, peach, and mauve. The Tempo Series ♀ offers a wide colour range, including shades of red, orange, and violet. The New Guinea Group of hybrids has bright flowers and bronze or variegated leaves. These are upright plants, suitable for the centre of a basket.
☐ to ❊ ◈

Lantana camara
Spreading evergreen shrub with compact cultivars. These plants, which flower from late spring to late autumn, are suitable for the edge of baskets. The small flowers, packed in dense rounded heads, are in a wide colour range, with bicoloured effects, for example pink and yellow, in the same flowerhead. L. montevidensis, another shrubby species, that trails slender, flexible stems, has mauve to violet flowers.
☐ ◈

IMPATIENS TEMPO SERIES ♀

Lobelia erinus
Plant trailing lobelias, which flower indefatigably throughout summer, in the sides and at the edge of hanging baskets. In the Cascade, Fountain, and Regatta Series the flowers are in shades of blue, violet, red, and pink, or white. The violet-blue 'Sapphire' has a white eye. There are also compact cultivars.
◨ ✳

Lotus berthelotii ♀
(Coral gem, Parrot's beak)
The silvery effect of the leaves, composed of grey-green narrow leaflets, held close to the lax trailing stems, makes this a good foliage plant for planting in the sides and at the edge of baskets. There are also beaked orange-red flowers in late spring and early summer. The flowers of the similar L. maculatus ♀ are more yellow.
◧ ◉ to ✳

Mentzelia lindleyi
(Blazing star)
Summer-flowering annual with wispy green foliage

LOTUS BERTHELOTII ♀

LOBELIA ERINUS 'SAPPHIRE'

studded with five-petalled yellow blooms that are fragrant at night. Best planted at the edge of baskets.
◧ ✳✳✳

Mimulus
(Monkey flower)
Loose and spreading plants, grown as summer annuals, with showy tubular flowers that flare to a broad mouth. Spotting or blotching often adds to the effect of bright reds, oranges, and yellows. Plant at the edge or in the centre of the basket. 'Viva' has yellow flowers with red splashes. The Magic Series includes some pastel shades.
◨ ✳✳✳

Myosotis sylvatica
(Forget-me-not)
Sprays of small, yellow-eyed blue flowers complement larger flowers in spring displays. Grow as a biennial and plant at the edge or in the centre of the basket. 'Music' has large flowers. The compact Victoria Series extends the colour range to white and pink.
◨ ✳✳✳

Nemesia strumosa
Bright, prettily shaped flowers in profusion in summer for the edge and centre of the basket. Some have veined or bicoloured flowers. The Carnival Series has a wide colour range. 'KLM' has flowers in blue and white.
◧ ✳

Nicotiana, dwarf hybrids
(Tobacco plant)
Grown as summer annuals for their numerous flowers, in some cases fragrant, which are tubular but open to a starry mouth. The dwarf kinds are suitable for planting at the centre of hanging baskets. The Merlin Series has flowers in white, lime-green, and shades of pink and purple.
◨ ✳

Origanum 'Kent Beauty'
Semi-evergreen shrubby perennial with arching stems and bright green rounded leaves. In summer the small pink flowers are almost hidden by long-lasting bracts in delicate shades of pink and green. Best at the basket edge.
◧ ✳✳✳

ORIGANUM 'KENT BEAUTY'

PELARGONIUM 'APPLE
BLOSSOM ROSEBUD' ♀

Pelargonium, ivy-leaved
Like the zonal pelargoniums,
shrubby evergreen perennials,
but the stems are trailing and
carry fleshy ivy-shaped leaves
and a long display, from
summer to autumn, of single
or double flowers. Plant at
the edge or in the sides of
baskets. The single flowers of
the red 'Decora Impérial',
carried well above the foliage,
are clean cut. 'L'Elégante' ♀,
with variegated leaves, has
silvery single flowers. 'Tavira'
has cerise-red semi-double
flowers. 'Yale' ♀ is a blood-
red semi-double.
🔲 ◈

Pelargonium, zonal
Classic container plants
flowering non-stop in
summer. These are shrubby
evergreen perennials that are
grown annually from cuttings
and, in some cases, as in the
Pulsar Series, from seed. Plant
in the centre of the basket.
The clustered flowers are
single (eg 'Paul Crampel'),
double, cactus-flowered
(eg 'Brockbury Scarlet'), of
rosebud shape (eg 'Apple

Blossom Rosebud' ♀),
or starry, as in the Stellar
pelargoniums (eg 'Bird
Dancer' ♀). The colour range
includes many shades of red,
pink, and orange, and there
are clear whites. Fancy-leaved
kinds, such as 'Flower of
Spring' ♀, have boldly
marked leaves.
🔲 ◈

Petunia
The pastel and brightly
coloured hybrids are
mainstays of summer
container gardening. The
slightly sticky plants are
bushy to spreading and
produce prodigious quantities
of soft-textured trumpet-
shaped or double flowers for
months. The large-flowered
(Grandiflora) petunias, some
with ruffled flowers, are less
weather resistant than the
smaller-flowered (Multiflora)
kinds, such as the Mirage
Series, some of which have
veined flowers. Petunias that
make lax trailing stems are
suitable for the sides and,
even better, the edge of
baskets. The Supercascade
Series has large flowers in
white, or shades of blue, pink,
and red; the Wave Series, with
smaller flowers, comes in pink
and purple. The Surfinia
Series, available only as plants
grown from cuttings, is free-
flowering, weather resistant,
and vigorous.
🔲 ✳

Portulaca grandiflora
(Rose moss, Sun plant)
Fleshy-leaved sprawling
annual producing satiny
single or double flowers in
white, or vivid shades of pink,
purple, red, and yellow during

summer. The Sundance
Hybrids are semi-trailing.
Good for planting in the sides
or at the edge of baskets.
🔲 ✳

Primula, Polyanthus Group
Clusters of primrose-like
flowers standing above
rosettes of heavily veined
leaves add colour to late
winter and early spring
displays. Polyanthus are
usually grown as biennials.
Plant at the edge or in the
centre of the basket. In the
Cowichan Series, the velvety
flowers come in a range
of rich and subtle colours.
The Gold-laced Group has
mahogany flowers edged with
yellow. There are vivid, even
brash, colours to be had in
the Crescendo Series.
🔲 ✳✳✳

Ranunculus asiaticus
(Persian buttercup)
Perennial, but usually
discarded after flowering in
spring and early summer. The
clump of deeply divided
leaves is topped by branching
stems carrying single or, more
commonly, double flowers

PETUNIA 'PURPLE WAVE'

of fine-textured petals that are densely but exquisitely packed. Plant in the centre of baskets. The flowers are white, or in shades of red, pink, and yellow. ▣ ✳

Rosa
Miniature roses, twiggy, with sprays of single to double toy flowers, come in a wide colour range appearing through summer and into autumn. 'Red Ace' has semi-double crimson flowers; those of 'Stacey Sue' are double and pink. Although vigorous, the modern ground-cover roses are lax growers and suitable for large baskets. Avon, a very pale pink, and Northamptonshire, a white, have semi-double flowers. ▣ ✳✳✳

Scaevola aemula
Flings out stiff spreading stems that bear numerous small fan-shaped flowers throughout summer. 'Blue Fan' and 'Blue Wonder' are variations on the standard blue-purple colour. Plant at the edge of baskets. ▣ ◈

SCAEVOLA AEMULA

TROPAEOLUM MAJUS
ALASKA SERIES

Solenopsis axillaris
Starry narrow-petalled blue, sometimes white, flowers stud bushy to spreading flimsy plants throughout summer. Grow as an annual, using as a filler with more bushy plants. ▣ ◈

Tagetes, dwarf hybrids
(French and Signet marigolds) Summer-flowering annuals producing numerous long-lasting flowerheads in shades of yellow, mahogany, and orange. Plant French marigolds, such as the Disco Series, at the edge or in the centre of the container. The Gem Series of Signet marigolds, good at the edge of baskets, has fine foliage and neat flowerheads. ▣ ✳

Thunbergia alata
(Black-eyed Susan) A twining climber, grown as an annual, that adapts well to be treated as a trailing plant. Throughout summer it produces chocolate-centred orange or yellow flowers. ▣ ◈

Thymophylla tenuiloba
(Dahlberg daisy, Golden fleece) In summer, bright yellow flowerheads enliven lax plants with ferny foliage. Plant at the edge of baskets. ▣ ✳✳

Tropaeolum
(Nasturtium) Climbing and trailing annuals with nearly circular leaves, wavy at the edge, and spurred flowers in shades of pink, red, orange, and yellow throughout summer. Plant at the edge of baskets. The semi-trailing Gleam Series has semi-double flowers in a good colour range. The Alaska Series, more dwarf and bushy, has cream-marbled leaves. The Whirlybird Series, also dwarf and bushy, has flowers that stand well above the foliage. 'Hermine Grashoff' ♥, a trailing bright red double, is propagated from cuttings taken in late winter or early spring. ▣ ◈

Verbena
The best suited to hanging baskets are the spreading and branching hybrids planted at the edge. They weave among other plants, posing heads of clustered small flowers in a pleasingly random way. Those to raise from seed include the violet-blue 'Imagination' and 'Peaches and Cream', cream to orange. 'Showtime' offers a mixture of colours, including red, pink, and purple. Verbenas raised from cuttings include 'Lawrence Johnston' ♥, a bright scarlet, and 'Silver Anne' ♥, with fragrant pink flowers fading to white. ▣ ✳ to ✳✳

FLOWERS FOR SCENT

VIOLA 'BOWLES' BLACK'

Viola
(Pansies and Violas)
A range of pansies with subtle or bright velvety flowers, some with face-like markings, freely produced over spreading clumps of heart-shaped leaves. They are grown as annuals or biennials. Many are summer-flowering, including the Clear Crystal Series and Crystal Bowl Series, in single colours, and the strongly marked bicoloured Joker Series ♥. Winter-flowering pansies – in reality they are often in their prime in spring – include the Universal Series ♥ in a broad range of colours, and the small-flowered Jewel Series, in blue, purple, and yellow. In summer, small-flowered violas of great character, some perennial, but others usually grown as annuals or biennials, look sprightly beside the large-flowered pansies. 'Bowles' Black' is velvety dark, almost black, with a golden yellow eye; 'Johnny Jump Up' is purple and yellow; and 'Prince Henry' is a dark purple.
◨ ❊❊❊

All of the following have scented flowers; include them in baskets by windows or doors where you can enjoy their fragrance.

Brachyscome iberidifolia
(Swan River daisy)
A lightweight annual, usually spreading, that bears small daisy flowerheads for months in summer. They are usually purple-blue and fragrant, but the colour range of some selections, including the Splendour Series, extends to pink and white. Use to fill gaps around the edge of baskets.
◨ ❊

Heliotropium
(Cherry pie, Heliotrope)
Compact and shrubby, usually with wrinkled dark leaves, heliotropiums are grown as annuals for their dense heads of fragrant small flowers in shades of mauve and violet. Plant in the centre of the basket. 'Princess Marina' ♥ has strongly scented deep violet flowers.
◨ ❊

Hyacinthus
(Hyacinth)
The spikes packed with waxy fragrant flowers are stocky and upright but, combined with laxer plants, make handsome candles – pink, blue, white, yellow, or red – in the centre of spring displays. Plant bulbs in autumn.
◨ ❊❊❊

Lathyrus odoratus, dwarf
(Sweet pea)
The sweet pea, an annual flowering throughout summer if picked regularly, has dwarf forms. Plant to fill and spill out of the basket. The Bijou Group, only lightly scented, has ruffled flowers in shades of pink, red, and blue, or white.
◨ ❊❊❊

Narcissus, dwarf hybrids
(Daffodil)
Spring bulbs with upright foliage and stiff stems bearing single or several trumpet or cupped flowers, mainly in shades of yellow, but also with white flowers. Early-flowering dwarf hybrids, planted in autumn, brighten the centre of containers in late winter and spring. 'Jack Snipe' ♥ has reflexed white petals and a lemon-yellow trumpet. 'Tête-à-tête' ♥ is long-lasting, carrying 1–3 small, rich yellow trumpets per stem.
◨ ❊❊❊

BRACHYSCOME IBERIDIFOLIA

FOLIAGE PLANTS

THE PICK OF THE ARCHING and trailing foliage plants that do well in hanging baskets are worth growing on their own. Some have interesting but subordinate flowers that add to their appeal. The virtue of many is that they give body to mixed plantings while spacing out flowers that otherwise would have an overwhelming effect because so densely packed.

Adiantum capillus-veneris
(True maidenhair fern)
An evergreen or deciduous fern of exceptional elegance, worth being shown on its own in a basket. Glossy black leaf stalks support arching sprays of triangular segments. The sprays fall over one another to create a layered effect of delicate green lace.
☀ ✻✻

Artemisia stelleriana 'Boughton Silver'
Sprawling evergreen perennial with soft silvery grey leaves cut into rounded lobes. The felted layers spill over and disguise hard edges of containers. The yellow flowers, seen in late summer, are insignificant.
✿ ✻✻✻

ASPLENIUM SCOLOPENDRIUM 'CRISPUM'

Asplenium scolopendrium ♈
(Hart's tongue fern)
An evergreen fern with leathery, strap-shaped fronds clustered to form an upright, glossy, bright green shuttlecock. 'Crispum' and 'Undulatum' have fronds with wavy margins. In the Cristatum Group the fronds have crested tips. Plant in the centre of the basket with shade-tolerant trailing plants at the edge.
✿ to ☀ ✻✻✻

Cyrtomium falcatum ♈
(Japanese holly fern)
Evergreen or deciduous fern with spreading, glossy, dark green fronds composed of segments resembling holly leaves. The upright growth of this distinctive fern makes it suitable as the centrepiece of a green display.
✿ to ☀ ✻✻

Euonymus fortunei 'Emerald Gaiety' ♈
Young plants of the evergreen shrub *E. fortunei* make useful foliage fillers in containers – after a season in a basket they can be moved on to make useful plants in the open garden. White margins to its bright green leaves give 'Emerald Gaiety' ♈ a fresh sparkle; in winter, the leaves are tinged with pink.
✿ ✻✻✻

HAKONECHLOA MACRA 'AUREOLA' ♈

Glechoma hederacea 'Variegata'
(Variegated ground ivy)
The lilac-mauve flowers count for little, but the long trailing stems of this handsome evergreen or semi-evergreen perennial are prettily strung with kidney-shaped leaves, their scalloped margins brightened by irregular white splashes.
✿ ✻✻✻

Hakonechloa macra 'Aureola' ♈
Grasses rarely feature in hanging baskets, but this is worth planting on its own so that its bright yellow leaves, darkened by a green stripe, can arch out freely. In autumn, the leaves take on a red tinge.
✿ ✻✻✻

Hedera helix

(Common ivy, English ivy)
Small-leaved versions of the
common ivy, a tough and
highly adaptable evergreen,
are decorative whether
trailing or climbing. Plant in
the sides of baskets or trail
over the edge. The three-
or five-lobed leaves vary
considerably in shape and
colour, many selections
having white, cream, or
yellow variegation. They
are true year-round plants,
whether growing on their own
or as part of seasonal displays.
Variegated examples in white,
cream, and yellow include
'Glacier' ♀, 'Eva' ♀, and
'Goldchild' ♀. 'Duckfoot' is
an appealing green-leaved ivy
that takes its name from the
shape of the leaf.
◧ to ▣ ✳✳✳

Helichrysum petiolare ♀

A lax evergreen shrub widely
grown as an annual in mixed
container plantings. The
stems work their way among
other plants, the woolly grey-
green leaves giving body in a
colour that goes well with

soft shades and is also an
ideal foil for bright hues.
There are creamy flowers
from midsummer. Variations
on the species are also useful.
'Limelight' is bright lime-
green, and 'Variegatum' has a
cream edge to shades of grey-
green. Trim back stems if they
become overwhelming.
◧ ✳

Heuchera micrantha 'Palace Purple' ♀

Jagged metallic purple-red
leaves make a dark clump for
the centre of a basket. In early
summer this perennial bears
sprays of tiny creamy flowers,
which are followed by pink
seed heads. Other heucheras
with dark or marbled leaves
make unusual foliage plants.
'Snow Storm', which requires
shade, has scalloped white
leaves that are margined and
speckled green.
◧ ✳✳✳

Lamium maculatum 'White Nancy' ♀

One of several variegated
forms of a sprawling
perennial with nettle-like
foliage. In this case, ice-white
flowers match the silvered
leaves, which are outlined in
green. Stems thrust their way
through other plants, the
foliage adding their cool tone
to mixed plantings.
◧ to ▣ ✳✳✳

Lysimachia nummularia 'Aurea' ♀

(Golden creeping Jenny)
A low-growing evergreen
creeper with bright yellow
flowers in summer. Its main
value in containers is the
foliage, the oval to round
leaves, trailed on long stems,

HELICHRYSUM PETIOLARE ♀

being yellow to yellow-green.
The yellow colour is strongest
in full sun.
◧ ✳✳✳ to ✳✳

Pelargonium, scented-leaved

The flowers are usually small
but the foliage, aromatic
when brushed or lightly
bruised, is often highly
ornamental. Use in the centre
of a basket and keep plants
bushy by pinching back
growth. 'Lady Plymouth' ♀,
which has mauve flowers,
has nicely cut leaves with
a cream margin and a scent
of eucalyptus. 'Old Spice',
compact and bushy with
small white flowers, has grey-
green softly textured leaves
that are spicily aromatic.
◧ ◈

Plecostachys serpyllifolia

Sometimes described as a
small-leaved, lightweight
version of *Helichrysum
petiolare* (see left), which is just
what it looks like. This shrub
is usually grown as an annual
in summer for its silvery
foliage. Plant to trail from the
sides or at the edge of baskets.
◧ ✳

LAMIUM MACULATUM
'WHITE NANCY' ♀

Plectranthus forsteri 'Marginatus'

Upright then trailing plant that has rich green aromatic leaves with a white scalloped margin. The small tubular flowers are white or pale mauve. This perennial, sometimes grown as a houseplant, is commonly treated as an annual. *P. madagascariensis* 'Variegated Mintleaf', which is also trailing and with white variegated leaves, is grown in the same way. The crushed leaves smell of mint.

🔲 ◈

Senecio cineraria

An upright evergreen shrubby plant usually grown as an annual for its silvery grey felted foliage. The grey-green

PLECTRANTHUS FORSTERI 'MARGINATUS'

leaves of 'Cirrus' have an irregularly toothed or jagged edge. 'Silver Dust' ♀ has nearly white woolly leaves that are fretted with deep cutting.

🔲 ✱✱

Tolmiea menziesii ♀

(Pick-a-back plant)
In early summer there are spires of greenish white flowers, but the foliage of this evergreen perennial is more important ornamentally, the leaves being maple-like and hairy. And there is a surprise: young plants develop on mature leaves. The pale green leaves of 'Taff's Gold' ♀ are mottled cream and yellow.

🔳 to ◼ ✱✱✱

Trifolium repens 'Purpurascens Quadrifolium'

A form of the creeping perennial white clover. The four leaflets that make up each shamrock leaf have purplish chocolate centres edged with green.

🔲 ✱✱✱

PLANTS TO GROW FOR THEIR COLOURFUL FOLIAGE

When used imaginatively, foliage can play the same ornamental role as flowers. Make the most of its many shades of green, variegations in cream, yellow, and gold, and rich colours, such as purple and vivid red.

Brassica oleracea

(Ornamental cabbage, Kale)
Curled and wavy margins and elaborate cutting add complex ornamentation to rosettes of leaves in shades of red, pink, and green, or white. Their shape is uncompromising, but these are handsome plants to view from above in low-hung autumn or winter baskets. The Osaka Series has

rounded heads of frilled, bluish green outer leaves and centres in pink, red, or white.

🔲 ✱✱✱

Houttuynia cordata 'Chameleon'

A perennial that can stand on its own or be mixed with other plants. There are spikes of tiny flowers with white bracts at their base, but all attention is focused on the heart-shaped leaves in green, cream, and vivid red.

🔲 ✱✱✱

Solenostemon

(Coleus)
The soft nettle-like leaves, sometimes deeply cut and lobed, are strikingly patterned, shades of pink,

red, yellow, and brown combining with pale and dark green. The Wizard Series makes compact bushes.

🔲 ◈

SOLENOSTEMON

EDIBLE PLANTS

T HE BEST EDIBLE PLANTS to try in containers are ornamental as well as yielding crops. Strawberries and tomatoes are the most productive of the fruits and remain attractive for a long period. Herbs give good value, the removal of leaves and sprigs for the kitchen being a kind of light pruning.

ORIGANUM VULGARE '*AUREUM*' ♀

Marjoram, golden wild

The yellow to yellow-green leaves of *Origanum vulgare* 'Aureum' ♀, a bushy perennial, make a bright accent among other plants. 'Aureum Crispum' also has yellow foliage but is more lax and suitable for the edge of a basket.
🔲 ✳✳✳

Mint, pineapple

The combination of creamy white and green of *Mentha suaveolens* 'Variegata' adds a crisp freshness to the centre of summer hanging baskets. It has a fruity scent.
🔲 ✳✳✳

Parsley

The tightly curled rich green leaves are ornamental in containers, planted with other edible plants, or with flowers, and make a tasty and attractive garnish for many savoury dishes. Grow as an annual and plant at the edge of baskets.
🔲 ✳✳✳

Rosemary, prostrate

An upright evergreen shrub, but a sprawling version, *Rosmarinus officinalis* 'Prostratus', with the same narrow and aromatic leaves, makes a manageable plant with stems trailing over the edge of the basket. There are pale blue flowers in late spring and early summer.
🔲 ✳✳

Sage

The common sage is too large for hanging baskets, but *Salvia officinalis* 'Tricolor' ♀ is less vigorous, and its aromatic leaves are grey-green with an irregular creamy margin and purple-pink flushes. Plant to form part of the crown.
🔲 ✳✳

Strawberry

Attractive low plants with flavoursome fruit dangling from beneath the arching foliage. The best in partial shade, and pretty among ornamentals, are the small-fruited alpine strawberries, such as 'Mignonette'. In full sun try ever-bearing types, such as 'Aromel' and 'Calypso'.
🔲 ✳✳✳

Thyme

Numerous low-growing shrubby thymes are strongly aromatic and in summer carry dense heads of small flowers, usually purple-pink. *Thymus vulgaris* 'Aureus' and 'Silver Posie' are respectively golden and white-variegated kinds. More sprawling kinds are good at the edge of baskets. Most have pink to purple flowers. *T. serpyllum* 'Annie Hall' has pale flowers, and *T.* 'Doone Valley' has dark leaves with yellow splashes.
🔲 ✳✳✳

Tomato

Several kinds are well suited to trail, and in a sunny spot the ripening fruit of those, such as 'Tumbler', a compact cherry tomato, can be very decorative.
🔲 ◈

THYMUS VULGARIS '*SILVER POSIE*'

INDOOR FLOWERING PLANTS

To get the best results from house and conservatory plants, grow each in its own container. Unless otherwise indicated, these plants prefer a position in full light. When the climate is mild enough, plants can be grown outdoors, even if only in summer, and then most do well in light shade for part of the day.

Achimenes
(Cupid's bower, Hot water plant)
Bushy to spreading perennials with wiry stems carrying trumpet-shaped flowers throughout summer and into autumn. Start the tuber-like rhizomes into growth in early spring. Named hybrids cover a wide colour range. 'Peach Blossom' has soft peach-pink flowers. 'Purple King' is a deep red-purple.

Browallia speciosa
(Sapphire flower)
Dwarf kinds, grown as annuals, make low spreading plants with blue, violet, or white flowers giving a long summer season. Examples such as 'Blue Troll' and 'White Troll' can be raised from seed in late summer to flower in winter.

Campanula isophylla ♀
(Falling stars, Italian bellflower, Star-of-Bethlehem)
Stems trail, but the starry blue or white flowers of this perennial are upward facing. It is worth planting on its own for its long summer season, but a good pairing of blue and white can be made combining, say, 'Stella Blue', which has violet-blue flowers, and 'Alba'.

CAMPANULA ISOPHYLLA
'STELLA BLUE'

Catharanthus roseus ♀
(Madagascar periwinkle, Old maid)
Flat-faced flowers, opening out from slender tubes, are in white or shades of pink and red, sometimes with a red eye. The Pretty In Series includes dark and light flowers. These shrubby plants, at first upright and then sprawling, flower from spring to late summer.

Columnea 'Stavanger'
(Norse fire plant)
Trailing stems clothed in small glossy evergreen leaves are bright in spring and summer with the scarlet of numerous trumpet flowers. Sometimes has a sprinkling of flowers at other seasons, too.

Hoya lanceolata subsp. bella ♀
In summer waxy white flowers with red-violet centres form rounded clusters on the trailing or arching stems of this perching shrub. Their sweet scent is penetrating. Full light to ▣ ◈

Jasminum polyanthum ♀
White flowers in spring and summer are strongly scented. Stems of this vigorous evergreen climber may grow to 1.8m (6ft) and can be encouraged to twine up the supports of its container or left to trail.

Kalanchoe manginii
The branching and drooping stems of this succulent perennial are loaded with

CATHARANTHUS ROSEUS
PRETTY IN SERIES

bell-shaped red flowers in spring. *K.* 'Tessa' ♀ is a brighter red.
☗

Nopalxochia
(Orchid cactus)
Epiphytic cacti with drooping strap-shaped stems bearing showy flowers in late spring and early summer. Colours range from white and yellow to shades of pink and red. 'Gloria' is a vivid pink. Full light to ◩ ☗

Saintpaulia
(African violet)
Most African violets have very short stems but there are trailing kinds, with rosettes of leaves on extended stems. Singles have five-petalled flowers, sometimes fringed or ruffled, and there are semi-doubles and doubles in shades of pink, blue, and purple, or white. 'Fancy Trail' ♀, a double, has pink flowers, and 'Starry Trail' is a double white.
☗

SCHIZANTHUS PINNATUS 'HIT PARADE'

Schizanthus
(Butterfly flower, Poor man's orchid)
A showy annual, which makes an upright bush and is good for spring displays. The orchid-like flowers – mainly in pink, purple, red, and yellow – are marked and spotted. For hanging baskets use dwarf kinds such as *S. pinnatus* 'Hit Parade'.
☗

Schlumbergera × buckleyi ♀
(Christmas cactus)
This epiphytic cactus is one of the brightest flowers of winter. The stems, made of flattened leaf-like segments, bear at their ends bright magenta tubular flowers with reflexed petals.
☗

Streptocarpus
Clusters of tubular flowers, five-lobed at the mouth, are borne in succession in spring and summer. The stems of the large-flowered hybrids are upright, but some of the smaller-flowered hybrids are lax and sprawling. They come in shades of blue, purple, and pink, and white.
Light shade ☗

Streptosolen jamesonii ♀
(Marmalade bush)
Normally a scrambling shrub, but in a basket it makes a lax bush, which carries many clusters of yellow and orange flowers throughout summer.
☗

ORCHIDS FOR BEGINNERS

Although the flowers are bizarre and exotic, suggesting steamy tropical conditions, some orchids can be grown successfully in a conservatory or well-lit living room. Grow the two described in slatted wooden boxes, using an orchid compost.

Coelogyne cristata
A winter- and spring-flowering epiphytic orchid that does well as a houseplant. The sprays of fragrant white flowers, with conspicuous orange marks, arch over elegantly from a hanging container.
☗

Dendrobium nobile
An evergreen epiphyte that is a good beginner's orchid and a very distinguished plant. The waxy fragrant flowers are predominantly pale pink, very variable in their colouring, but with the white lip having a maroon mark.
Full light to ◩ ☗

COELOGYNE CRISTATA

INDOOR FOLIAGE PLANTS

MOST INDOOR FOLIAGE PLANTS benefit from regular misting. Unless otherwise indicated, they need bright conditions; during the summer, provide light shading to prevent scorching. Again, many can be grown outdoors in mild climates, if only in summer; ideally, place them in a slightly shaded position.

CHLOROPHYTUM COMOSUM

Asparagus densiflorus 'Myersii' ♀
(Asparagus fern)
Arching stems are densely clothed with green leaf-like needles. Another ornamental asparagus with arching growth, also known as the asparagus fern, is the half-hardy *A. setaceus* ♀.
❖

Begonia
B. rex and a large group of its hybrids are evergreen with large, nearly heart-shaped and pointed leaves that are handsomely marked; white or silver areas usually surround a dark centre. The colour range includes shades of pink, red, maroon, and brown, as well as green. The overlapping leaves arch out to hang over the edge of containers. There are sprays of pink flowers,

usually in summer. If moved outdoors in summer, they are best in light shade.
◨ to ◼ ❖

Ceropegia linearis subsp. **woodii** ♀
Widely spaced heart-shaped leaves dangling on slender stems. The upper surface of the fleshy leaves is marbled silver, while the underside is purple. In summer, there are small pink flowers.
❖

Chlorophytum comosum
(Ribbon plant, Spider plant)
The variegated forms are much-abused houseplants but at their best, when allowed plenty of space in a hanging container, are truly impressive, with the central clump dangling a family of plantlets. 'Vittatum' ♀ has white or

CISSUS DISCOLOR

cream central stripes; 'Variegatum' ♀ has cream to white leaf margins.
❖

Cissus discolor
In warm conditions a slender climber or eye-catching plant trailing to 1.2m (4ft) with heart-shaped velvety leaves. The upper surface has silver markings painted on deep green while the underside is maroon. Full light to ◨ ❖

Epipremnum aureum ♀
(Devil's ivy, Golden pothos)
A strong evergreen climber, but the less vigorous variegated forms are attractive trailing from containers. 'Marble Queen' has heart-shaped dark green leaves that are marbled and flecked with creamy white.
❖

Ficus pumila ♀
(Climbing fig, Creeping fig)
An evergreen climber that keeps its juvenile foliage if allowed to trail, which it will to 75cm (30in) or more. The heart-shaped to oval leaves are glossy and prominently veined. The creamy markings of 'Variegata' give a light effect. Full light to ◨ ❖

Sedum morganianum ♀
Best planted on its own so that the ropes of fleshy overlapping leaves hang

TRADESCANTIA FLUMINENSIS
'ALBOVITTATA'

unencumbered. This is an
evergreen perennial with
waxy blue-green foliage and
small red flowers.
✿

Senecio rowleyanus
(String of beads)
Plant on its own to get the
effect of masses of bead-
like balls spilling out of a
container. The bright green
leaves of this succulent
perennial are almost spherical
and its flowerheads are white
and purple.
✿

Tradescantia
T. fluminensis 'Albovittata'
has foliage with a striking
contrast of green and white,
the variegation running along
the leaves. A close relative,
T. zebrina ♀, has dark leaves
with two broad silvery bands
and an underside that is red-
purple, while 'Purpusii' has
deep bronze-purple leaves. All
are perennials and attractive
planted alone or in mixtures,
even in outdoor summer
schemes in light shade.
✿

INDOOR FERNS

Ferns are aristocrats among
foliage plants, the delicate
patterns of their fronds
showing infinite variations.
To get the most from these
attractive plants, place in
well-lit positions but out
of direct sunlight, and
maintain a humid
atmosphere by misting
them regularly.

Blechnum tabulare ♀
This evergreen fern makes
an impressive clump of
sterile and fertile fronds.
The genus includes several
other highly ornamental but
less hardy ferns, among
them *B. brasiliense* and
B. gibbum. Allow their full
development by growing
these ferns as single
specimens in a display.
❋❋

Davallia canariensis ♀
(Hare's foot fern)
The furry rhizomes that
escape the confines of

NEPHROLEPIS EXALTATA
'BOSTONIENSIS'

PLATYCERIUM BIFURCATUM ♀

a container, such as a slatted
wooden box, give this
deciduous or semi-evergreen
fern its common name. The
fronds are much cut,
triangular, and leathery.
▨ ✿

**Nephrolepis exaltata
'Bostoniensis'**
(Boston fern)
A tolerant houseplant and
an impressive evergreen
fern when grown on its
own and allowed to form
a large clump. The fronds
arch over, creating a layered
effect around a central
crown.
Full light to ▨ ✿

Platycerium bifurcatum ♀
(Common staghorn fern)
Branched leathery fronds,
mid- to deep green, arch
out and hang down from
a humus-gathering nest.
This variable fern is always
impressive when grown on
its own.
Full light to ▨ ✿

INDEX

ACKNOWLEDGMENTS

Picture research Cathie Arrington

Special photography Peter Anderson.
The baskets on pages 9, 12, 29, 31, 32, 33 and
43 were created by Malcolm Hillier for his
Container Gardening (Dorling Kindersley 1991)
and *Container Gardening Through the Year*
(Dorling Kindersley 1995); the baskets on pages
25 and 30 and on the front cover (centre) were
created by Gay Search for her *Gardening
Without a Garden* (Dorling Kindersley 1997).
Photographs by Matthew Ward.

Illustrations Karen Gavin, Gill Tomblin

Index Hilary Bird

Dorling Kindersley would also like to thank:
All staff at the Royal Horticultural Society,
in particular Susanne Mitchell, Karen Wilson,
and Barbara Haynes at Vincent Square.

The Royal Horticultural Society
To learn more about the work of the
society, visit the RHS on the Internet at
www.rhs.org.uk. Information includes news
of events around the country, a horticultural
database, international plant registers, results
of plant trials, and membership details.

Photography
The publisher would also like to thank the
following for their kind permission to reproduce
their photographs:
(key: t=top, c=centre, b=below l=left, r=right)

Garden Answers/Emap Active: 34c
Garden Matters: 9b, 23r
Garden Picture Library: John Baker back cover
c, 17b; Lynn Brotchie 10r; Brian Carter 20r; John
Glover 8r, 23l; Neil Holmes front cover cl, 11bl;
Howard Rice 14; Friedrich Strauss 2, 6, 15b;
Ron Sutherland 4br, 19t; Juliette Wade 22l & r
John Glover Photography: Front cover tl, 5bl,
11br, 16l, 17tr, 52
Harpur Garden Library: Designer Richard
Hartlage front cover bl, 11t; Maggie Gundry 18l
Andrew Lawson: Back cover tr, 7, 15tl, 16r,
17tl, 18r, 21l & r, 62
Clive Nichols Garden Pictures: Vale End, Surrey
24
Photos Horticultural: Back cover tl, 10l, 56b
Harry Smith Collection: 81, 12t, 15tr, 20l